CEMETERY
CHESS

Also by Sandy McIntosh

CEMETERY CHESS
SELECTED AND NEW POEMS

Sandy McIntosh

Marsh Hawk Press
East Rockaway, NY 2012

Many thanks to my editor and friend, Thomas Fink
and to my wife and partner, Barbara

12 13 14   3 2 1 First Edition

Marsh Hawk Press books are published by Poetry Mailing List, Inc., a not-for-profit corporation
under section 501 (c) 3 United States Internal Revenue Code.

Versions of the following new poems have been published in these journals:
The Patterson Literary Review: "Ravenous"; *Barrow Street:* "Innocence," "Reconstruction of a
Lost Poem by Armand Schwerner"; *Red Ochre Lit:* "A Lecture from the Bartender at Grand
Hotel, Oslo"; *Otoliths:* "Sestina: Against the Painted Corpse," "Ten Engulfed Cathedral,"
"Military School Thug"; *Marsh Hawk Review:* "from *Four Problems of Translation.*"

Cover photo: the Grand Cafe, Grand Hotel, Oslo, circa 1890
Author photograph: Anne Hall Cover design: Claudia Carlson
The text of this book was set in Adobe Garamond Premier Pro.

Library of Congress Cataloging-in-Publication Data

McIntosh, Sandy
  Cemetery chess : selected and new poems / Sandy McIntosh.
    p. cm.
  ISBN-13: 978-0-9846353-6-8 (pbk.)
  ISBN-10: 0-9846353-6-X (pbk.)
  I. Title.
  PS3613.C54C46 2012
  811'.6--dc23

                              2012012827

Marsh Hawk Press
P.O. Box 206, East Rockaway, N.Y. 11518-0206
www.marshhawkpress.org

CONTENTS

from *Between Earth and Sky* (2002)

from *The After-Death History of My Mother* (2005)

from *Earth Works* (1970)

Progression for the Burial of President Eisenhower

I

Eisenhower, "the man who withstood,
died quietly today. He was 78.
At his bedside, his wife and dog.
Technicians removed, the remaining cameras,
shut down the lights,
folded the walls and moved backstage.

II

All over the country,
file cabinets are opened, charts read.
In the White House, President Nixon
inserts the yellow punch card
which cancels all his appointments and begins the program
of recorded music.

III

In Europe, the bodies of world leaders are dusted,
their clothes pressed. They are carried into the airplanes.

IV

Eisenhower is washed. His eyes are removed,
their lids sewn shut. His guts are excised,
his face erased and a new one applied.
He is given a final coat of wax,
packaged into the coffin and loaded into the
hearse.

V

On the day of the funeral the hearse
moves accurately to the program.
Under the roads, agents of the C.I.A.
are pumping the earth. Tiny salty

drops of water emerge from the road
in a token of suffering.

Behind the hearse, a dark army marches.
Flecks of dead skin settle quietly
to the ground.

AMERICA BEFORE THE REVOLUTION

for General Curtis LeMay, in Vietnam

Sir:
How I enjoyed
your words last night
about this being God's war: I was so excited
that I didn't notice eating
my mother who had fallen into her own apple-pie.

ON THE SHINNECOCK CANAL

— for S. K.

Move closer. Let me loop this cord
about you.
It is good that you are asleep.
I will begin walking through your body soon.
It is a long walk, I promise.
I will be quiet.

Last night I walked through your eyes
with a lantern in each hand.

from *Which Way to the Egress?* (1972)

SONG ABOUT MY HAIR

When my hair grew long
it grew hammers and axes.
When my hair grew long
it grew wild.

When my hair grew long
it grew nails and scissors.
When my hair grew long
it butchered my eyes.

My hair was the hair
of horses and trees.
My hairs were the heads
of thousands of people.

My hairs were the bones
of many small animals.

My hair was a carcass
bleached by the sun.

Snow fell inside me
when my hair grew out.
Light entered backwards
when my hair grew out.
I went blind by the sun
when my hair grew out.
I was bleached by the constant
internal eye.

Now, I've cut off my hair.
Now, I've cut off my hair
to build the new world.

BOSWELL AND JOHNSON, TO NAME TWO

They are friends because,
well, look here: There is a bird
who rides the craters of an alligator's
back. A parasite, but also beneficial
to the alligator.
In the bird's wing is a tick,
also there for a purpose.
On some part of the tick
stands an imagined being: he has a big TV eye
and a small divine body.
In his hands is a wheel, as if on a ship.
He turns the wheel to the left .
below him the alligator rolls.

FOUND POEM: THE DYNAMO

from The New York Times, September 10, 1908

A living storage battery is E. G. Atloy
lives with his widowed mother.
He is a human magnet, with the electric properties
of a dynamo engine.
A metal filling had been put in
one tooth,
and when the boy came home
he picked up the knob
used to connect an electric fan
and thrust it into his mouth.
His head jerked slightly.
The fan began to revolve
and to buzz
frantically.
The mother was frightened
and feared witchcraft.
The boy seemed pleased.
A piece of iron held in the boy's hand
became highly magnetized.
A hammer with an iron handle
attracted tacks
at four feet.

He has red hair,
large freckles
and blue eyes.
He feels only an agreeable
sensation.

THE GERIATRIC EXPRESS

I am thinking of starting a newspaper,
the GERIATRIC EXPRESS,
with obituaries on the front page,
and news of the world in the back
(by which time my readers will all be asleep).
It is a trick like one I saw
where the top card keeps moving to the end of the deck
behind the magicians back,
and suddenly there are no more cards left
and the magician looks into the audience
for a long time, and then falls asleep.
The curtain descends on an empty house,
while out in the street
an empty armed newsboy
is hawking the GERIATRIC EXPRESS
to no one at all,
until he, too, falls asleep, or,
grunts, wakes up in front of a family album
shuts down the lights and goes off to bed.

from *Monsters of the Antipodes* (1978)

ROSA-ROSA GAVE ME A KISS
(AND WHAT HAPPENED THEREAFTER)

Rosa-Rosa gave me a kiss which covered up my lips
and slid around my chin
and jumped into my shirt
on its two spider legs.
I tried to grab that awful kiss
but it hid in my armpit, and I could not grab it
when it ran down my back.
So I screamed, and stunned it with my scream
when it got caught in the belt of my pants,
and I threw it back in Rosa-Rosa's face.
It hit her mouth, but not exact,
and it stained her red like a spider bite.
Rosa-Rosa looked at me so sadly
I put my arms around her
and she leaned against my shoulder.
And as we stood that way, her lips parted
and her teeth bit into me.
And ever since, whenever I kiss some woman,
those lips hiss and spit at her,
and sometimes the woman runs away.
And that is why I do not get
too many kisses
anymore.

THE ARNOLD SCHOENBERG MONUMENT

The new science found a use
for musical devices. Dissonance
made the best fuel for tanks and rockets.
A tone-cluster could fire a human to the moon
and back again in moments.
The Twelve-tone system of composition
was studied by the Ministry of War.
The name Ernst Krenek was whispered in mystical circles.
Soon it was found that machines themselves were not necessary.
The only thing people had to do to go from place to place
was to hum a minor seventh and close their eyes.
To get back, they had to sing a major second.
A perfect fifth got the shopping done
while a retrograde row slowed the aging process.
In the capital city the new science unveiled the Schoenberg Monument.
It is carved from white marble and it shows the figure of Schoenberg at the center
holding the Tablets of the Law. Behind him and leaning slightly
over each shoulder are Berg and Webern
with angel wings and cherubic smile.

DECEMBER NIGHT

Dear Aunt, when the first snow fell tonight
I thought of you sadly.
It was because, as the snow
covered your grave
I knew it had ended your last battle
on this earth.
Your grave has become as white
and anonymous
as the graves of my grandparents
that surround you.
Each winter the snow rubs against the graves
until all below are rubbed out.

Dear Aunt, I see you now
as I have never seen you,
but as I think I must each year hereafter:
only once, and in the winter,
and under the light
of the first falling snow.

from *Endless Staircase* (1991)

VAMPYRE CAMEOS

for R. B. Weber

The young vampyre
makes homely women beautiful
by his love. He showers them with gifts.
He dances in weird, fire-lit imagination.
He thanks his good fortune,
but soon becomes empty,
vacant as a swimming pool in autumn.

The vampyre in middle age
makes homely women homelier.
His gifts become cloying: bits of string,
his false teeth. He dances before them,
but his victims retreat. He persists,
but his thoughts wander. His eyes
lose hypnotic power.

The senile vampyre
is captured by homely women
and taken in hand. They mend his dress suit.
They brush his top hat. They stuff
his hollow body with rags and make him dance
the new steps. The vampyre believes his love
has made him young. He longs to wander
back alleys, but his lovers sew him
into a banner which they hang
above the castle door. There he flaps
like a bat every night in the rain,
flaps himself into shreds,
then flaps no more.

THE GENERATOR

"What are you thinking?" asked my wife as we lay around on a Sunday. "It's something I remembered about my father and me, and why I always worry about my art."

On my ninth birthday I had invented the Generator down in my basement laboratory. It was a white cardboard box with dials and wires in front and a toy tractor motor in the back that made the special Generator sound. My friends from school came to my birthday party. Those I wanted to impress I took downstairs to the basement after ice cream and cake. "This is my Generator I invented!" I announced. And I turned the dials to ON with one hand while slipping the other behind to turn on the motor.

What a sound it made!

But my friends only laughed. "That's not a generator," they said.

"It is, it is!" I pleaded. I could not believe they would not believe me. "Go ask my father."

"Okay," they said. "Let's go ask your father."

We stood at the bottom of the stairs. "Call your father," they ordered.

He appeared at the top on the landing.

"Daddy," I asked. "Isn't it really a Generator?" My eyes searched my father's face for the secret code, some way to let him know my dilemma. Help me please, Daddy, I begged him on all the silent frequencies.

He was looking at us. Couldn't he see my friends standing behind me, their faces smoldering red, saliva on their fangs?

"Well," my father finally answered. "It certainly generates something."

Oh no, I thought. Oh no.

My friends laughed. I protested. "You don't understand..." But they laughed, and then it was over.

"Anyway," I said to my wife. "I think that is why I wonder so much about my poems. Am I fooling myself again? Can people see inside me where phony motors grind? I wonder and I look hard, but the most I can ever get from the eyes of other people is, *yes, they certainly generate something.*

SQUARING THE CIRCLE

Take me to lunch, she said.

Why should I? he said.

Because I touched your dick, she said.

That was for your benefit, he said.

I've heard that before, she said.

Hundreds of times, I'll bet, he said.

But I never touched such an old one, she said.

Because you hang around schoolyards, he said.

You probably can't keep it up for an hour, she said.
Men never can, she said. They come too fast, she said.

With you, they want to get it over with, he said.

With my luck, she said, you'll turn out
to be a forty-year old premature ejaculator.

Thanks a lot, he said.
Don't mention it, she said.

That's a terrible poem, she said.

Well, I wrote every word we said, he said.

And you made your lines funnier
than mine, she said.

But you win all the same
in the end, he said.

Well. I'm not saying another word
you can steal, she said.
And, goddamn it, put down that pencil when I'm talking.

The Social Function of Poetry

He had read Eliot's *The Social Function of Poetry,* Ezra Pound's letters, and the essays of William Carlos Williams. He was ready to fight for poetry's place. He was teaching poetry to children in the public schools, and wanted to convince them that poetry offered something powerful for their lives.

Meanwhile, a friend from graduate school called. The friend worked for a public relations firm and needed some genuine Irish poetry for a film about Dublin. The poetry, said his friend, must extol the beauty of the land, the vitality of the people, and the rapid growth of industrial production.

He spent an afternoon searching the library's anthologies. Not surprisingly, he found nothing answering the requirements. All Irish poetry was depressed. In the end, only one appeared reasonably upbeat. It began: *Thank God, I've left Ireland forever!*

His friend told him not to give up. He needed the material; his job depended upon it. He named the famous Irish-American television actor contracted to read the verses in the film. "Go back to the library," begged his friend. "You've got to help me out of this jam."

He tried another library without success. In the end, he decided to forge it, to create an ancient Irish poem to order. To his surprise, it was easy: All he had to do was imagine an ancient village scene and voice it in Yeatsian diction. In a short time, the rhymed stanzas appeared fully-formed, like photographs in a chemical bath.

In the deep musical voice of the film's famous narrator, the verses and pictures became powerfully fused. The first scene: quiet, leafy trees. Swans preening upon the rustic pond. The second scene: The camera pulls back. The pond is ringed by a cobble-stone square. Dubliners of all ages, happy and vigorous, stride by. The third scene: The camera pulls back again. The street is at the center of a modern industrial city. Within the blue skies of this diorama, smoke curls contentedly from chimneys.

His friend was delighted, the project completed, the sponsor happy, and the film honored at a film festival.

Later, he returned to the his teaching job, contemplating poetry's place.

WEDDING SONG

for Joan Griffiths and Kurt Vega

Let us grow together
and be known as the Strange Thing, or the Living Rock.
And let bright creatures
come forth from our caves.
Let us become craggy
and be called grandmother and grandfather.
And let your name be mine
and mine be yours,
and let our secrets stay secrets.
Let us become inseparable
and spin through space
and be anonymous as a comet
that appears once a thousand years.
And when we are seen rolling
through the air, and when someone asks our name,
let him wander and ask others, and let him wonder,
but let him never find out.

OF STRANGE LANDS AND PEOPLE

— for Justine Rydzeski

"I don't want to play this piece anymore," my favorite piano student said to me. "It's dead baby music. When I play it, all I think of is dead babies!"

It was "Of Strange Lands And People" by Robert Schumann. "All I think about when I hear it is Schumann throwing dead babies off a bridge. And then I see them bunched together on the ground like plastic dolls!"

I could not argue against her. She was rightly intuitive: There is a weakness in Schumann that abides the hundred years between his times and our own; that stretches like telegraph line connecting his heart at one end, and the music we play at the other. When we tap on the keys, the coded message gets through.

Schumann went insane. He threw himself off a bridge into the River Seine. He died later in an insane asylum with his bed-clothes bunched about him.
Dead baby music.

A Reliquary

I.

She was the talented daughter of my aunt's first piano student. It was her birthday. She was 10. I was 6. My aunt took us to the Metropolitan Opera. My mother bought her a gift in my name. I wanted to give her something from me, personally, but kept putting it off. After the opera, I told her I'd hidden it under the snow.

We dug and dug,
but the gift
was nowhere.

II.

Brilliant, tall and blonde, she became engaged to the high school football hero.

He perished in a car accident.

She left for Vassar. Her letters to me on philosophical questions sailed over my head.

III.

She married a French lawyer. They moved to Paris where she taught at the Sorbonne.

Her husband fell down
the apartment stairs and died.

His best friend consoled her. They became engaged. Vietnamese, he flew to his parents in Saigon.

Two years passed.
The war continued.

No word
from him.

IV.

Working at the United Nations as a translator of multiple language, she became attached to an authentic great-nephew of the last Czar.

They moved
into a mansion.

V.

They had twin girls. Her husband seemed healthy, not prone to accidents.

"Now I can relax."

One daughter turned out to be a genius, the other, mentally challenged, needing a special school to accommodate this anomaly. She would sell the mansion and move to the City.

She suffered from lupus.
Incurable.

VI.

An old friend of the family told me the rest: She'd died in horrible pain. Her Russian husband, grief-stricken, had wandered off. Her twin daughters now lived with their ancient grandmother.

VII.

Around that time,
my wife and I divorced unpleasantly (although
I remember how
we cried in each other's arms with the knowledge
that something we had borne had died).

Philosophy in the new century
must teach us joy
in the abandonment
of the useless search for meaning.

Sleeper Awake

My dead aunt returned.
I hid beneath the window.
This had been her house;
now it was mine.
She wandered across the street.
No one answered the door.
I saw shadows
against the curtains.
Awake from a long dream, my aunt was home.
Where was everyone?
The sleeper awake,
the living in darkness beyond.

Endless Staircase (1)

Of my brother's death
I imagine two things:
I see him skidding and dipping his toes
combing the flirtatious waters.
I understand the temptation
to slip over the edge,
to roll up the eyes, to be gone, to dissolve,
to disintegrate like a pearl in wine.
And I see myself on the morgue's endless staircase,
the rancid wind pushing against me,
pushing with such force
I cannot reach the door.
And, indeed, a year later,
I see myself descending those stairs,
as if this descent had become
my whole road.

Endless Staircase (2)

I had agreed to identify my brother's body at the morgue because there was no one else except my mother to do it. There was no way out of this errand. I had asked my friend, Kurt to come along as a favor of ultimate loyalty and friendship. He'd agreed.

Queens County Hospital complex is perpetually busy. All sorts of people walk the streets or pass through the buildings. Some have their arms in slings. Others walk with crutches or ride wheelchairs. Some are bent over, walking slowly. A few gesticulate vigorously and direct traffic or debate invisible antagonists.

The Mortuary operates in building "H" of the complex. It stands at the end of the road, next to the laundry. Inside there are several bolted doors marked "No Admittance" and two open office cubicles.

I stepped into the first and waited for the clerk to finish her long telephone call. Then I spoke the horrible words: "I'm here to identify my brother's body."

The clerk pointed without interest to the next office. "Over there," she said.

I turned and repeated what I had to say. The young woman behind the glass partition asked me to sit and wait. She, too, was on the phone.

"I'm sorry, Mr. Rodriguez," she was saying. "The body you're looking for isn't here. Why don't you try the Manhattan Medical Examiner? Oh, I see. Well, how about Jacoby in the Bronx? Yes? Well, I'm sorry, we can't help you. Um-hmm. You too. Good luck."

She returned to the cubicle where I sat with my friend.

"May I see your identification?"

I fumbled for my driver's license.

"Your relationship to the deceased?"

I told her.

"Did the deceased use drugs?"

I told her which ones.

"It is necessary at this time," she said, "to identify the body."

I imagined the bolted doors opening, the tables of the dead I'd visit now, their faces, bodies, a tableau of horrors of violent endings.

But the clerk only opened an envelope. She withdrew two photographs. "You'll identify the body by looking at a photograph."

She looked intently at them, holding them with their blank backs facing me. Then chose one and turned it decisively, as if it were a reproachful Tarot card.

It pictured my brother, his head only, wrapped in a white sheet, his eyes closed, his face bruised. Blood on his lips and chin. The sneer, the public swagger he wore, was gone. I thought of my mother's words that morning and echoed them: "That poor little boy."

To Kurt, the corpse looked naïve, surprised to find itself dead.

In the car driving home I said, "I'm going to tell my mother that my brother looked peaceful."

Of course, that wasn't true, but that's what I told her.

ENDLESS STAIRCASE (3)

I was visiting my brother's bedroom.
He was hiding under the mattress.
His hideout smelled of sweat.
He was cataloging business cards collected on a recent trip to Europe.
I felt it was my duty
to tell him he was dead.
Officious, self-appointed scum! I reproached myself. But who else would tell him?
"You're dead, Donny," I said.
He looked into my eyes; he
couldn't avoid them, trapped where he was.
"How did it happen?" he asked.
"An overdose," I told him. "Like Lenny Bruce,"
"I see," he replied. "I'll just stay in here
by myself a little longer, if you don't mind."
"Ok," I said. "Go ahead. Do whatever you want."
I stood up and took a deep breath.
At last he knew the truth. At last
he had listened to me.

from *Between Earth and Sky* (2002)

BLISTERED HANDS

I was in a fine restaurant wrestling an old man
for possession of a coffee pot.
"Give it to me now!" the man whimpered,
trying to force my fingers apart.
"It's bitter," I shouted at him. "Undrinkable!"

The boiling coffee splashed and scalded our clothes.
I could crush you to death this instant,
I remember thinking.
I squeezed the old man's arms
and felt his bones splinter: desiccated insects.
I stepped back and looked at us both:
our dress clothes stained, our faces blistered.
What a waste, I thought.
To kill this old man
when I myself never drink coffee.

THE OCCASION OF DESIRE

Marilyn Monroe threw herself onto the sand
as we walked along the beach.
"Look," she teased, "I've found the fool-proof way
to drive men wild!"
She began to strip off her clothes, one layer at a time,
writhing in the sand like an eel.
"Each time I take something off," she explained,
"I wait a little longer before taking off the next.
By the time I get to the flesh,
every man will be insane with desire."
She removed piece after piece,
arousing me as never before.

When she reached the last, she called:
"Come into my arms, lover."
I looked at my watch: I was late for work.
"I'm sorry," I answered. "I have to go to work."
She looked into my eyes with such silent anguish,
I knew she would be dead by morning.
All I could do was show her my watch.
"See?" I pointed out sadly.
"I'm late already."

BLACK MASKS

I thought I recognized my parents in an old porno film.
That must be my father, I thought, in his dark Methodist suit,
driving his car along the dusty road,
grinning like a devil in horny expectation.
The world in black and white, grainy and silent,
accelerates by the car windows. My father
sees a woman by the side of the road near the woods.
She sticks out her thumb and he leaps on the brakes:
it is my mother in her light summer dress
who leers at us through the windshield.
I notice her small hands.

My father beckons my mother inside
and they fumble against the rigid seats.
Then, with her dress up to her neck
and his pants around his ankles,
they begin to screw.
I am watching my mother and father
in the back seat of a car,
and they are wearing black masks.

IMPOSSIBLE SITUATION

It was a horrible meeting:
The principal warned me "Don't you teach poetry
to those children!"
"But, but..." I stuttered.
"And don't give me any crap
about 'sensitivity'!" he screamed.

Abandoned, I stood under a tree
and pulled down my pants,
but women were watching from the windows.
I decided to take a cab home to mother.
The driver said he too was a teacher.
He said he'd do me a favor: he'd take me to a subway.
He steered the cab down the subway stairs,
bumping along, until we reached the platform.
"I don't know what to do," he said,
getting out to ask for help.

"Nothing like this has happened before," one witness declared.
"A taxi on a subway platform?" declared another.
"It's an impossible situation!"

I could have left then, taken the first train home,
but I stayed on. He was a colleague, after all,
and I could never abandon him
to an impossible situation.

MEETING AN OLD FRIEND AT A LECTURE

A small leaf had settled on your shoulder,
stuck to the threads of your sweater.
I had been about to pick it off, but you bent forward,
suddenly attentive to the speaker,
and your wild gray hair flapped
and rustled as if in a wind.
I thought how much like an old tree you had become,
and I would not remove your only leaf.

from The Landlord's Confession, or *Louder Desperation*

1. Elliot, or *Flight*

After losing his job as an advertising copywriter when the department store chain went out of business, Elliot was tired of thankless work. He'd saved his money. The rent on his fisherman's cottage was low, so he decided he'd spend his time perfecting certain inventions.

"I think I can get by for ten years without a job."

A reserved man, he kept his lights off on Halloween Night so "the strange man who lives all alone" would not trouble the neighborhood parents.

After a few years he ran short of cash and found work with the Census Bureau. His job compelled him to walk through the neighborhood asking householders personal questions, such as "Who lives in your house?" and "What do you do for a living?" and "How much do you earn?"

One afternoon I found him hanging his wash on the clothesline. I asked how the census was coming. He waved me over, his finger to his lips. "I had to quit that job," he whispered. "You see, the Mafia was after me."

"How do you know?"

"I had an argument with one of them. He wouldn't answer my questions. I told him he had to; it was the law. So he threw me out of his house. Now I'm certain he drives back and forth at three in the morning sending me messages over his car radio."

"What messages?"

"He says he's going to kill me."

"When?"

"Any day now," he answered.

In October that year, a hurricane uprooted a tree in front of Elliot's house. Its heavy branches pierced the roof, coming to rest inches above his bed. Elliot was unhurt but convinced it was not nature that caused the invasion; it was the Mafia. "I'm going to have to go away for awhile," Elliot announced. "I'll keep in touch."

He asked me to take care of his house, but there was no need to go inside: he had shut everything down and the bills were paid. There was nothing for me to do. A month later I received a letter: Elliot was in Montana. The snow was falling, he wrote. He was staying with a friend who owned a log cabin. "He's got horses, and we ride every morning mending fences. Please accept this rent check. Hope everything is fine with you."

The next month, his rent arrived with a postcard from Hawaii that featured the ocean and several Hawaiian women wearing flower garlands. "I'm here in Hawaii. The girls are treating me nice," he wrote.

A month later he was in New Orleans. "Here's the rent, right on time," he wrote. "Looking forward to Mardi Gras!"

And so, for the next six months, Elliot sent his rent from a different state. He seemed to be having a great time. Stuck at home with my chores, I envied him.

That summer, Elliot's mother arrived, as she did each year, from her home in the Virgin Islands. I was getting ready to do some roof work on one of the houses when she invited me inside for coffee. Sitting at the kitchen table was Elliot.

"Welcome back," I greeted him.

"Thanks," he said with an unusually shy smile.

"Elliot has something to tell you," his mother said to me.

"Well," he began. "You remember all those letters I sent from all the different states? The truth is, I really didn't go to all those places. I was really here all the time."

"How is that possible?" I asked. For almost a year his house had shown every sign of being unoccupied.

"Well, it was real easy," he answered. "During the day I kept to myself. I'd wake up at sunrise and by the time the sun was setting I'd be ready for bed. Once a week I'd set the alarm clock for 3 a.m. and go shopping at the all-night supermarket. See? No problem."

In a way, it sounded an almost healthy way to live. "But how did you get to mail your letters from all those states?" I asked.

"Easy, again," he answered. "I've got people I play chess with by mail all over the country. I just sent them the letters and asked them to mail them for me."

A few weeks later, Elliot gave me his notice. His mother was leaving for the Virgin Islands and she was going to take Elliot with her. "Momma's going to help me get away from the Mafia," said Elliot.

"Yes," said his mother, sadly. "Away from the Mafia."

2. Margaret, or *The Spider's Web*

Margaret, a retired Marine major, spied on her neighbors through the slats in her screen porch. She would call me to recite the outrages: "Walter's been nuding about in his backyard, again," she would report. Or, "Fred in the rear house had three young boys to visit him last week. I wonder what he does with them in there?" Or, "That Evans woman made an awful face when she passed my house today."

Each time, I'd promise to warn the offenders not to do it again. Otherwise, Margaret kept to herself, "improving the house," she would say, and never inviting anyone inside.

At eleven o'clock one night, during an intense electrical storm, I was hosting a dinner party for friends. The storm exploded overhead and the electricity went out. We rushed to the window, and all the houses on the street were dark. The telephone rang; it was Margaret.

"You'd better come quickly," she demanded in shrill whisper. "Little Timmy next door has murdered his father!"

"How do you know?"

"I heard the shot," she said. "I thought everyone on the block could hear it!"

"That was thunder."

"No," she countered. "That was a gun. Call the police."

Five minutes later she called again. "Have you called the police?"

"Not yet."

"Well you'd better do it soon. I can hear someone moaning in their basement."

I put the problem to my friends at the dinner table. We agreed on a plan. We would break into Timmy's house and search for bodies. We grabbed flashlights and raincoats and forced open the rear window of the house. Inside, we felt our way along the walls, playing the flashlight around corners, convinced we were about to stumble over something dead. But we searched the attic, the main floor and the basement without finding a corpse. Finally, there was only one room left to search: the bathroom. Inside, the shower curtain was closed. While the others watched from the doorway I flung it open: Nothing. No one. The house was empty. I banged on Margaret's porch door.

"Don't make so much noise," she whispered. "I'm right here."

I told her there was no corpse in the house next door.

"He's removed it," she said with finality. "He dragged it out the other way. You'd better call the police."

I was weary. "Why don't you call the police?" I asked her.

"Oh, not me," she said. "I don't want to get involved."

I learned several days later that Margaret had not been entirely wrong: Timmy had been home during the storm, but had left before we broke into the house.

"Maybe she heard me playing darts," Timmy suggested. "I was having a good time. I yelled when I hit the bull's-eye."

"And your father's okay?"

"Sure," Tim said. "He's never home; he works nights."

Several months later, Margaret announced she would be moving to Florida to live with relatives. "There's more regular people down there," she assured me. "I've had enough eccentricity up here to last a lifetime."

After she'd moved out I inspected the house. Without her boxes, towels and clothes blocking my view, I discovered she had installed one hundred seventy-three electrical outlets in the walls. I called the electrician, who stared silently at Margaret's snarl of wires in the basement and said, "I can't imagine why this house hasn't burned to the ground."

THE OPERATION

We met at a party one night in Amagansett.
She was celebrating her divorce. She kept shouting,
"Come on! Let's be happy!"

It was late. I was drunk. I wanted to go home,
but she insisted we go dancing.

"I'm too tired," I told her.

"What are you? Sixty? Seventy? A hundred?"
she taunted. "Is it baby's bedtime?"
"Alright," I said. "Let's go."

Several of us got into the big car out back.
She climbed onto the hood.
"Who do you think you are? Zelda Fitzgerald?"
someone called out.
We arrived at the dance club and she slid off.
"I might have to be sick a little later on," she confided.

I had to borrow money to get us in the door.
We danced and drank.
She offered to let me stay with her for the night.
"I've got some Champagne and a canopy bed,"
she declared.

Her house was a dark outline on the beach.
"We have to be awfully quiet," she told me.
"We can't wake my daughter."
We stumbled through her living room without lights,
feeling our way with toes and fingers.
She flicked the switch. Her bedroom was brilliant:
damask curtains, an Aubusson carpet,
and lacy material bridging the posts of her bed.
We drank the Champagne
and undressed with the lights on.

Her bed was like an operating theater:
I could see the veins in her breasts and thighs delineated
as if on an x-ray.
We began to caress, but she pulled away.
"Wait," she said. "What am I doing?
I can't do this. It's too soon.
You'll have to leave."

She gathered my pants and shoes
and pushed me out of the room. "Be careful," she warned.
"Don't wake my daughter."
I crawled along the floor looking for the back door.
"God damn it, I'm lost!" I whispered,
hoping she would hear.
An hour later I found my way out.
I drove home, Brahms blaring loud on the tape deck
keeping me awake.
I was furious.
She made me believe
I was the most attractive man at the party, but I was
compromised.

Several years later, I met her at an art opening.
I had had a long time to rethink that night.
I no longer hated her.
It wasn't her fault. I had come to admire her courage
to make a difficult decision, given the circumstances.
"You don't remember me," she began hesitantly.
"Yes. Yes I do," I replied.
"I just wanted to tell you how sorry I was about what happened."
"Oh no," I said. "Don't worry about it."
"Well, thank you," she said, relieved.
"But do you know something
that's always bothered me?"
"What?" I asked.
"I was so wrapped up in myself,
I never even asked your name."
"Ah," I replied, nodding my understanding,
my tolerant indulgence.

Of course, I'd never bothered to ask hers, either.

FOR A MAN WHO LOST HIS WIFE

Living under the same roof
with a wife you no longer loved,
you kept to separate spaces, a locked door in between.
You'd chosen for yourself the smaller room,
with bed, stove, desk and bookshelves
crowding you into the center.
"Let her have the rest of the house," you told me.
"It's what she's always wanted, anyway."

And now she's dead, and you continue to live
in your overcrowded room, as if your wife were still living
behind the door that's locked.
"I'm too lazy to move," you tell me with a shrug.
"My things would be here and there.
Nothing would be in its familiar place."

On Mackinac Island I once saw pulling a wagon,
two horses who bit and kicked each other the entire journey
under the driver's whip. When I protested the cruel confinement
of creatures obviously at war with one another,
the driver laughed and later showed me how,
released into pasture and free to run wherever they wished,
the horses stayed together, biting and kicking the while,
the harness never the real binding,
circumstance never the actual whip.

New Year's Morning

After a late night I drive my friend, John,
to the cemetery where the family graves
are marked by monument.

I drive around
lost and hung-over.
I've been here so many times before.
Why can't I find it?
"I'm lost," I tell him.

"You're pathetic," says John.
"A man so lost he can't find
his own grave."

Between Earth and Sky

for Lanford Wilson

"Sandy was a prodigy," my mother, in old age,
tells her Florida friends.
"He was the youngest writer ever to win the prize—
only sixteen when the famous English author
P.G. Wodehouse took him under his wing...."

What is this? I ask myself. I don't remember
anything of the sort.

She goes on: "And Mr. Wodehouse published
his first book for him. And Sandy was—did I tell you? —
just fourteen, the youngest writer ever
to win the big prize!"

My mother is so full of pride,
and her new friends make approving sounds
in a good-natured, absent-minded way, smacking their lips.
There was a time when I would have corrected her
right then: "No, Mother," I would have said. "That isn't true."
But I've known for some time she's been going
round the bend, her memory dissolving in dementia.
It is only a surprise to find
she has been busy rewriting our scripts with happy endings!
No longer am I the son who failed to prosper
in business or the law. She is happy
I am nothing but a writer. And I am happy too:
for that is all I ever wanted to be.
Still I feel the tugging of the cord that connects this mother
and son (though the mother is 84 and the son is 50.)
I know I must let go soon, for I am heavy on the earth,
and she has become as light as wind,
the sky calling her as if she were a kite.

But perhaps not yet:
That night, in a dream, I am in P.G. Wodehouse's home.
He has invited me to visit his library.
I have been here before—many times before!
I remember the low ceilings, the bookcases—
so many thousands of books. And Wodehouse's own novels,
just where they should be. Everything so familiar;
Wodehouse has indeed taken me under his wing,
my mother, correct after all. How could I have doubted her?
So, for now, the mother and son remain united.
Between earth and sky, we meet in dream.

THE BIRD KILLERS

for M. A. V.

"I tell you, something is very wrong,"
my mother on the phone from Florida complains.
"Last week they put a dead squirrel in my car.
Then they nailed a dead bird to the screen door.
But last night!
Last night I heard them crawling all over my roof!"

"Whom did you hear, Momma?" I ask in my quietest voice.
"My damn neighbors, of course!
Those maniacs. Scratching and crawling
on my roof all night—that's the limit!"

"Why do you think your neighbors
are crawling on the roof?" I ask.
"To get at the pretty birds in my backyard, of course,"
she answers, as if it were self-evident.
"They want to kill the little birds.
Why the hell else would they be climbing on my roof?"
Obviously her medications are out of whack.
"Are you taking your Prozac?" I ask.
"That stuff?" she answers. "It makes me giddy like an idiot.
I flushed the bottle down the toilet."
I call her doctor.
"I've got something else," he assures me.
He adds, "It's a magical drug.
The nagging parent takes it,
but it's the child that feels the relief."

Next time I call she's as agitated as ever,
complaining about the neighbors again.
"But Al and Mildred," I tell her.
"They're in their eighties.
How could they be climbing on your roof?"

"You think I'm a senile old woman, don't you?
Believe me. It's them. They hate my birds."
Wasn't the new prescription supposed to calm her,
to end all this nonsense?
"Give it a few more weeks," her doctor tells me.
"It's bound to kick in soon."

In December I fly down for a visit
with no idea what I'll find.
But when my mother meets me at the door
she's all smiles and welcoming kisses.
Her house is spotless, and she's set the table
for Christmas dinner.
"I've invited the neighbors," she tells me. "Al and Mildred.
Such nice people."
With silent thanks I realize the medicine's finally working.

Over cocktails, Al takes me aside.
"We've been having trouble with the fruit rats," he whispers.
"We've called the exterminator several times.
The last time, he looked over the fence
into your mother's yard.
He says your mother was throwing birdseed all over the lawn.
It's the birdseed that attracts the rats.
Do you think you could get your mother to stop doing that?"
I tell him I'll try, but I can't promise
my mother will change her ways.
"Yes, I know," he answers. "I've tried to talk to her myself."

Meanwhile, Mildred and my mother have been talking
about birds. Mildred says she can't stand them.
"They carry disease," she shudders.
I study Mildred, an annoying old lady with a smarmy smile
that the surgeon pulled too tight.
But my mother is radiant and absorbed in their conversation.
When finally the neighbors leave

my mother tells me it's been a wonderful Christmas.
She's tired now, though,
and we can clean up all the mess in the morning.

I go to bed thinking about my mother and her neighbors.
Maybe she wasn't so wrong about them, after all.
Maybe there was something real
amongst her hallucinations.
Then, as if in answer, I hear a sound above me,
something scuttling across the roof.

I'll be damned! I think. Could it be the goddamn neighbors?

But as I listen I realize what I'm hearing
isn't the clamber of humans,
but the clatter of a thousand little feet
seeking foothold in the roof tiles,
making chinking sounds
as they shimmy down the drain pipes.
They're racing each other to the backyard,
I surmise with sudden certainty,
because my mother has just this evening
sown the lawn with birdseed,
a Christmas treat for her pretty birds.

My Mother at the Audiologist's

My mother at the audiologist's
insisting she doesn't need a hearing aide.
"OKAY," I order.
"LISTEN AND REPEAT WHAT I SAY."
Directly behind her I shout, "NOW IS THE TIME
FOR ALL GOOD MEN
TO COME TO THE AID OF THEIR PARTY!"
She doesn't respond.
"DID YOU HEAR ME?" I demand.
"Of course I heard what you said," she answers testily.
"WELL, WHAT DID I SAY?"
"You said, 'The old lady is stone deaf.'"

My Mother Dreams of Her Parrot

A week before her heart attack
my mother dreams of her parrot.
"I had gone away and Pixie was so very sad," she tells me.
Now in the ICU, after a terrible night of emergencies,
I watch her as she sleeps, lifting her hands,
moving them gently through the air.
She could be dreaming of her parrot again, stroking his head,
scratching his banded feet, his clipped, grounded wings
that he's lifted for her.
Finally, her arms drop to her sides.
"Go on," she whispers. "Go."
And Pixie flies away.

from *The After-Death History of My Mother* (2005)

PRIVATE

On the way home from school I found a bundle of nudist magazines. I tore out some pages and hid them under my desk blotter. For days I studied them, amazed at the mysteries of pubic hair. I imagined myself in the adult world, and it seemed a strange land, compelling and lonely but full of possibility.

Later, I found the pictures on top of my desk. My mother had rummaged through my room, never saying a word, leaving the naked pictures there for me to know she knew I had them. I was never beyond her grasp. Private parts would never be private. She herself was a greater force of nature than even adulthood, and we both knew her name was Silence.

PASTRY

I miss my mother's pastry, thick with cream cheese and chocolate—the twelve-layered Dobos Torte she baked for my twelfth birthday! She never ate pastry herself. Instead, she'd stare at me, like a recovering alcoholic at a gin bottle. She'd joke maliciously: "Inside every fat boy there's an even fatter boy trying to get out."

"Yeah. And he's really pissed off," I told her when I'd guessed what she was up to.

There were years when no one ate pastry. Mother listless, shrank into herself, until I brought home chubby Natasha They bonded, one lonely Eastern European to another. Happy now, my mother relit the oven.
Each day she'd feed Natasha fresh pastry, encouraging her with word and gesture, enjoying the scene—until Natasha, suspicious, vanished. Months later she returned, slim and pretty. She had a new boyfriend. They stayed the night.

Next day Mom was alone. "I couldn't get her to eat a thing," she lamented. "And all night, she and that boyfriend going at it like newlyweds."

THE HOSPITAL CHAIR

The hospital parking lot is empty.
My mother's in her favorite chair refusing to speak.
"Such a character," laughs her roommate.
"She touches you and tells you you are healed and may go home."
Her roommate hands me a pamphlet
with favorite quotations of my mother
assembled by the other patients:
a collection of libelous rumors concerning my wife and me.
One passage, supposedly from Jesus, reads:
No one knows what will happen
When I leave my tomb in the night
To touch you.

THE DEATH CHAIR

Mother died at home in her favorite chair.
Later, we moved her chair to our house,
setting it in the living room, hoping
it would find anonymity among other furniture,
no longer entrapping our morbid attention
when a hapless visitor sat in it by mistake,
squirming under our gaze, as though, perhaps,
he's done something to distress us.

THE PRODIGAL'S CHAIR

Yuki's father died. She was ten. She couldn't believe it.
"He's joined *Himitsu tan-tei,* the Secret Police,"
she shouted to anyone listening.
"He's away on a mission."

Thirty years later, her father shows up at her door.
She shouts to anyone listening:
"See? I knew it all along!"

Her father is home
but there is no room for him now.
Their habits have changed.
They'd sold his favorite chair.
He can't keep from getting in their way.
"You'll have to go,"
she finally tells him. "It can't be helped."

He collapses, sobbing like a child—
disbelieving, reckless, uncontrollable—
as if something he's been holding back
for thirty years.

THE WAKE-UP CHAIR

Margarita sits herself down in the wake-up chair.

"What can I get for you, madam?"

"A cup of coffee, strong and black!"

And then it's another day
signing her name again and again,
her handwriting a thread uncoiling,
a car wrecking itself by the side of the road.

Oh, the monotony, the boredom, of repeating one's own name!

She envies those who sign with an X
or those who only pretend:
dashing black contrails across the pages.
And then there's nothing left to sign,
and the waiter brings her a cup.

"Take it away," she tells him. "It'll only keep me awake."

CEMETERY CHESS

We lower my brother's coffin
beneath his monument.
Abruptly, mother hisses: "Look!"
Not twenty feet away,
another monument,
the grave of my brother's nanny.
"She wanted him for her own," mother whispers.
"Now she's got him."

A decade passes.
The game of Cemetery Chess progresses slowly.
Mother dies; her monument
erected midway between brother and nanny.
As we lower my mother down
I whisper to the nanny:
"Check."

I MET MY DEAD BROTHER,

hair glistening black,
he looked about nineteen.
"How did you get so young?"
He pointed to his backpack.
I protested it wasn't a backpack;
it was his corpse—I'd remembered it
from the coffin.
"You're mistaken," he smiled.
Then, waving his hand,
he walked off,
fading from memory.

Scotland

I want the haunted house to myself.
First, my dead mother appears. "I'm going to work."

I know she hasn't driven the car in forty years,
She looks okay, though a bit unsteady on her feet.
"All right," I tell her cautiously. "Go."

By the time my dead brother wanders in
I'm beside myself, trembling. "Why did I ever let her take the car?"

"Chill, man," says my brother. "Too much noise."

To my relief, mother appears at the door.

"How is the car?" I scream.

"The courts were closed," she answers.

"But what happened to the car?"

"The passport office wouldn't issue a passport."

"Did you have an accident with the car?"

"No," she tells me. "The car is fine."

"Well then, where is it?"

She looks blank—has she misplaced it? —
then beams with assurance. "Scotland."

THE AFTER-DEATH HISTORY
OF MY MOTHER

She showed up at my front door one morning
having walked away from the Alzheimer's institution.
She thought it was spring, but it was winter
and she had been sleeping in the snow.
I finally found another institution that would take care of her:
our public library, which had a small budget for videotape.
"As long as the money holds out
your mother can stay with us. We'll photograph her
from time to time, and you can watch her touching progress—
or regress or decline, as the case may be."

They invited me to my mother's latest screening each week,
and I watched her journey through whimsy, vagueness, petulant tantrums,
until she was finally silent—unwilling or unable to answer
the interviewer's questions.

Then I was told that the library's funds had run out
and my mother's project would be terminated.
I would never see my mother again,
since over time she had become an image on a screen,
and the library would pull the plug.

IGNATOW INTERRUPTS A DREAM

You were reminiscing about Ignatow, and I was dying to interrupt—I loved him, too, of course. I didn't interrupt because I had a sudden memory of making love in a dream only to be awakened by the actual person I'd been dreaming about who had been sleeping next to me, but was now shaking me to stop my terrible snoring.

And again, that was similar to another experience I had, this time at an academic conference at which eight of us read our papers on the poetry of David Ignatow. The man next to me had been happily reading his when in walked Ignatow, an unexpected guest.

The man whispered: "Now what do I do if he interrupts me to criticize? Why, oh why didn't I pick some dead poet to work on?"

Jim Tate sat next to a young woman on an airplane who was sobbing softly. He offered her a tissue. She explained that her father had died and she was returning home for his funeral.

Tate had been reading the newest David Ignatow. He gave the girl his copy to read.

"Thank you," she told him after they'd landed.
"He made me see something. I don't know quite what, but it helped a lot."

Ignatow, Hays, Ginsberg and I sitting on Hays' front porch. It was a quiet summer night in the Hamptons.

"We'd been having a musical evening at Alfonso Ossorio's, the night Jackson Pollack died," said Hays. "The sky was like tonight. I think someone was playing a jazz sax. I drifted off. Then Julie was shaking me. 'Wake up Hoffman,' she whispered. 'Look over there.' I looked and saw those evil lights of police emergency down at the end of the road."

"Are you sure?" asked Ginsberg. "I thought Pollock was killed on Springs Fireplace Road, that hairpin curve."

"Well," said Hays petulantly. "That's where we all were at the time. That's where

Alfonso Ossorio lived. Right after that curve."

"I didn't even live here then," said Ignatow.

"We weren't talking about you," muttered Hays.

That evening was long ago. Hays died first, then several years later, Ginsberg. Ignatow, never subtle in person, looked significantly at his wristwatch, then at me.

When Ignatow died he left me his watch.

POOR FITZ

Zelda said your penis
was too small,
so you complained
to your friend Hemingway,
and he agreed to examine it,
and did so—minutely—
in the toilet of a bistro
where you'd both been drinking.

Examination complete,
he pronounced it okay, really,
just the right size.

He could afford largesse
as he proudly visualized his own penis,
a great coiled thing
that lived at the bottom of the sea.

BRIDE OF THE MALL

I had been browsing the bookstore in our mall in a disconnected sort of way for some twenty minutes, my anxiety mounting over the absence of my wife of just two weeks. Wanda had been gone for quite some time and I was afraid she might have gotten herself lost. It was a big mall, after all, I'd begun to wonder if, since our marriage, instead of learning to better recognize each other, we had begun to forget who we were. I even had the apprehension that when she finally returned I would not be able to identify her.

I blame this confusion on our engagement and on everything that followed.

I don't know how it happened. So far as I was concerned, we had no designs upon each other except for the mild pleasure of each other's company—and that, not every day. We had been drifting without destination through the Mall one weekend afternoon when she tugged at my arm, interrupting my daydream. "Let's go into that jewelry store. They've got something there I want you to see."

I followed her into the store, and my eye was immediately drawn to the fine watch counter. "Don't dawdle," she scolded. She led me to the cabinet that displayed diamond engagement rings, objects that had never interested me, since I would never wear one. She pointed to a large diamond mounted on a filigreed band. "Isn't that gorgeous? Don't you just love it?"

"It's quite lovely," I said, trying to sound interested.

"I fell in love with it as soon as I saw it a few weeks ago." And then in a playful voice, "We're you thinking the same thing I was thinking?"

That was a hard one. "What were we thinking," I asked diplomatically.

"Oh, just that, you know, if we ever thought about getting married, this would be the ring you would buy for me."

Unexpectedly I entered a hazy dream "Certainly," I assured her with as much clarity and confidence as I could muster. "That would surely be the ring, if we were thinking about, you know, that... er, doing that."

She seemed genuinely happy, and I did not discourage her when she asked the saleswoman if she could try it on. To my surprise, the ring fit her finger perfectly, as if it had been made for her. "You see," she said modeling the ring before my eyes. "Doesn't it look pretty?"

Again, I felt I should assure her, and happily agreed that it looked superbly pretty.

She motioned me aside. "You know, darling," she began, and I quaked at the word 'darling', a name she had never called me before. "You know, a ring as pretty as that might be sold right away. Maybe, you know, just in case we ever decided we wanted to get married, maybe we should put a deposit on it, just so they'll hold it for us?"

I told her, cautiously, that that seemed the logical precaution to take, in the circumstances. But I was gasping for air, desperate to buy some time.

"Good," she told me. "I'd hoped you'd say that." She turned to the saleswoman who had been standing behind the counter waiting for Wanda, though there were other customers in the store needing attention. "Can we put a deposit on that ring?" she asked the saleswoman.

The saleswoman said yes, but only if we were planning to pay the balance within a few days. "Oh," Wanda said in disappointment and turned to me. "That's too bad."

I agreed that it was too bad, and contrived to put on a sad face.

"There is something else you can do," the saleswoman said after a moment.

"Yes?" Wanda asked.

"If you took the layaway option, you could leave a deposit on the ring now and take up to two years to pay it off. Would you be interested in that?"

I saw a chance to play the gallant, and immediately agreed that that was a good idea. After all, much can change in two years. It was a good way to buy time.

And Wanda seemed pleased. With her encouragement I allowed the saleswoman to charge a deposit to my credit card, with similar increments to be deducted monthly. I could always get my purchase price back, she assured me, if, for some reason, we decided not to take the ring. Wanda and I made reassuring sounds to the clerk, and then left the store for lunch.

"You know," Wanda told me over the French fries. "I've just been calculating the interest on that ring. It's going to be a lot, almost enough to buy two rings when we're finished paying it."

She showed me the calculations she'd been making on the back of the lunch receipt and I had to agree with her: the interest was indeed excessive, almost, usurious. "Too bad we don't have enough money to buy the ring right now," she lamented.

Her lament rubbed against my pride. Yes, it was indeed a great deal of interest to pay. So why not buy the ring now and keep it until—or if—we decided to go through with the engagement? I'd save a lot of money, and I'd hide the ring in my safety deposit box until the event. "You know," I told her. "I think you're right. Why don't we do this: why don't we buy the ring right now and put it away until we decide what we're going to do?"

Wanda appeared to think. "Yes," she said with a judicial air. "It's a lot of money to lay out for something we don't know will ever happen, but it is the right thing to do, financially. You're a good businessman, my dearest. Let's do it!"

So, we bought the ring, but instead of hiding it away, Wanda asked if she could wear it for a bit, at least until I drove her to her parent's home. The ring did look wonderful on her finger, and as we drove the twenty minutes to her house, we fantasized on what married life would be like for us.

It was an enjoyable trip. To our surprise, when we pulled up to the curb in front of her house, Wanda's family was standing there waiting for us. Wanda opened the car door and held up her left hand to show her parents. "Look what we've bought!"

"You're engaged!" her family proclaimed in joyous unison.

And so we were from that moment on.

What followed was, for me at least, a blur lasting several months. Wanda's mother, sisters, aunts and other female relations took over our lives. Happily for me—or, less unhappily—I was left out of most of the campaigns. I discovered early on this was to be all about Wanda.

The most vexing thing, aside from the marriage ceremony and reception (during which Wanda force-fed me repeatedly with sticky, sugary, wedding cake, among other outrages), was the necessity that Wanda and I play these curious roles: first, the Engaged Couple, and then the Married Couple. The misdirection inherent in this role-playing, I suggest, was the behavior that caused me to fear, as I stood there awkwardly in the mall's bookstore, that I would not recognize Wanda when she eventually found her way back.

In all, I probably remained abstracted, rooted to my spot, for an hour. When I woke, or came to, focused my eyes, I was gazing into those of a woman. "You look lost," said the woman. "Have I kept you waiting long?"

It was Wanda, or, at least, she seemed to be Wanda. "Are you alright?" I ached for some familiar cue to identify her.

"Yes," she answered. "Yes," I think I'm alright. It's just that I got lost looking for some gift to surprise you with...." She hesitated, then asked, "You are my husband, isn't' that true?"

"Yes, yes of course I am. And you are my wife?"

"Oh," she answered, initiating the first and last truly intimate moment we were to have. "Forgive me. It's only that I've been in such a haze since the wedding."

I sought to reassure her. "It's alright," I told her. "You and I are going to be alright."

However, this did not seem to assure her at all.

We left the store together, arm in arm. Yet, as we walked into the sunshine of the parking lot I asked myself, teasingly, if this woman I was with was, indeed, the real Wanda? Was it possible she was some confused stranger who had misplaced her own newly wedded husband and had come upon me in error? That I was a confused husband who had misplaced his newly wedded wife and, against all odds, accepted a substitute?

I asked myself these questions teasingly at first, then with mounting suspicion. And after these several years, I've come to believe the most radical answers. We were not the same people who first met, some taking pleasure in our company. Like the unfortunate children who wake from panicked dreams desperate to know if they had not been placed mistakenly with the wrong parents, Wanda and I have also been victims of a syndrome: the unconscious, hapless couple switched at the altar by forces beyond their understanding.

I suspect there are many like us.

My Hay(na)ku

(With Handy Pronunciation Guide for Public Performance)

Lorca!
His foot
in the doorway!

Pronunciation Guide:

"L" as second "l" in "Llewellyn"
"o" as "o" in "amoeba"
"r" as "r" in Southern US pronunciation of "cornpone"
"c" as fourth "c" in "acciaccatura"
"a" as "a" in "aesthetic"
"H" as "h" in "catachresis"
"i" as "i" in "poiesis"
"s" as second "s" in "sans serif"
"f" as first "f" in "afflatus"
"o" as second "o" in alternate spelling "encyclopoedia"
"o" as second "o" in alternate spelling "encyclopoedia"
"t" as first "t" in "attorney"
"i" as "i" in "poiesis"
"n" as "n" in "limn"
"t" as first "t" in "attorney"
"h" as "h" in "catachresis"
"e" as "e" in "eidetic"
"d" as first "d" in "addiction"
"o" as second "o" in alternate spelling "encyclopoedia"
"o" as second "o" in alternate spelling "encyclopoedia"
"r" as "r" in Southern US pronunciation of "cornpone"
"w" as "w" in "wrist"
"a" as "a" in "aesthetic"

NOTE: "Y" is pronounced "the the".

EILEEN R. TABIOS

"I really think you should title this poem 'Eileen R. Tabios'"
—*Eileen R. Tabios*

Eileen R. Tabios
Announced today
That her next book
Will be
5000 pages long.
In an unrelated development
Eileen R. Tabios
Announced
That she has acquired
A major interest
In International Harvester,
The only U.S. manufacturer
Of oversize poetry book forklifts.

It was learned
Early today
That Eileen R. Tabios'
Book for the next year
Will be
13,000 pages long.
In an unrelated development
Eileen R. Tabios
Announced
That she has acquired
San Francisco's famous
Coit Tower
Which she will turn
Into a library
Housing one large print
Version of her book.

It was learned
Early today
That Eileen R. Tabios
Has acquired large tracts
Of the Pacific Ocean
For an unknown purpose.
In an unrelated development
Eileen R. Tabios
Announced
That the number of pages
Of her future books
Will be counted
In leagues and fathoms.

It was learned
Early today

(continued next page)

Prof. Ferguson's Weekend

It has always been the author's cherished hope that the several techniques of observation, valuation and thought described in the foregoing, should at some future date find their application in the understanding of social problems beyond the confines of the academic world, and so to better us in our daily lives.

— James A. Ferguson, *Methodological Assessment Techniques for the Modern College English Department*

A well-cut lawn has always been central to the suburban neighborhood. While methods of lawn maintenance have changed over the past fifty years, careful observation has shown that three lawn-cutting paradigms remain dominant. These include the *Objective*, or Versa, the *Subjective*, or Nautilus, and the *Transactional*, or Aleatoric.

In the *Objective* method the operator begins at the edge of the lawn and pushes the mower straight ahead until she reaches the opposite edge. There she turns the mower 180 degrees either to the left or right as appropriate, in much the same way as a line of verse turns at its strophic conclusion. The operator commences to push the mower forward, cutting a parallel "furrow" of grass. In this way, the lawn to be cut is kept to the objective "outside" of the operator, and is never contained in any way, as it is in the subsequent method.

Those operators employing the *Subjective* method begin with their mowers at the edge of the lawn, cutting a straight path forward until they reach the opposite edge. In this fashion, the operator turns her mower only 90 degrees either to the left or right as appropriate, continues cutting a path to the edge, turns 90 degrees again, continues to the next edge, and so on until a rectangle is completed. The operator then turns the mower "inward," cutting ever-smaller rectangles, spiraling continually like the inward-turning chambers of the nautilus, until the cutting is complete. At this point, the operator is seen to be alone with her machine—and her contemplation—at the very center of the lawn.

The *Transactional* or Aleatoric method allows the operator to integrate her dedication to lawn cutting with her responsibility to the outside world. In this method, the mower may be positioned for beginning at any point. The operator then chooses to cut the lawn in any direction at will as she interacts with the terrain or with young children, dogs or neighbors who may distract her from the completion of an otherwise neat, geometric pattern. This method further allows for the completely aleatoric, unattended cutting of the lawn by a power mower, should the operator be called away to the telephone.

Professor Ferguson has made a careful study of the lawn mowing methods of his next-door neighbor. From his position of observation (a knothole in the fence that divides his property from his neighbor's), Ferguson recorded in minute detail his neighbors' struggle to mow his lawn on a hot summer's day.

Ferguson reports that his subject, although beginning with a strictly *Objective* approach, switched to the *Subjective* after he noticed Ferguson staring at him through the knothole. Each time his neighbor would pass his observation post, Ferguson notes, he would direct a sharp kick against the fence at approximately the level of Ferguson's eyes, at the same time shouting some imprecation against the observer that Ferguson fails often to specify. In the interest of his own strictly *Objective* criteria, Ferguson refused to acknowledge any of his neighbor's requests that he "get the hell out of there and mind your own fucking business."

Ferguson notes that as his subject reached the halfway point of his labors, he suddenly threw down his mower and resorted to his back porch, where he drank a great quantity of beer. Ferguson assumes that his subject had reached the end of his initial inspiration and was, in this way, retrenching for a new attack upon the problem.

After several hours Ferguson's neighbor once again returned to his lawn mower. Rather than repositioning himself where he had left off cutting, Ferguson reports that his neighbor again shifted paradigms, this time to the *Transactional*. Ferguson admits to being rather shaken as he realized that his neighbor had now aimed the mower at Ferguson, who continued to squat behind the fence, and proceeded to charge at him, yelling "Are you still there, you idiot?"

After staring blankly at the fence for some time, Ferguson's neighbor returned to the job and continued to push his lawn mower randomly about the lawn. After ten or fifteen minutes he apparently decided to abandon the project temporarily or, perhaps, forever. (Ferguson surmised this much after watching his neighbor fling the lawn mower repeatedly against the fence.) Ferguson's neighbor then disappeared into his house, reappearing after some minutes, and headed in the direction of Ferguson's own home.

While remaining where he was in a model position of objectivity, Ferguson noted that his neighbor was greeted at the front door by Ferguson's wife, whose gestures, especially her embraces, indicated that he was welcome to come in. After a short silence, Ferguson reports, a radio was turned on to a loud rock 'n roll station, and presently Ferguson observed his wife and neighbor dancing and laughing.

Such was Ferguson's dedication to the *Objective* method that he remained at the fence, even after the lights had been turned off in Ferguson's bedroom. It was necessary for the observation, asserts Ferguson, that he remain at his post, since it was possible that his neighbor might reappear at any time to finish cutting his lawn.

OBSESSIONAL

I open the door

and there's the famous poet,
Max, dancing
about: black hair, beard, fierce horses
eyes, chanting loudly
with the radio:

"Move bitch, get
out the way
Get out the way bitch, get out the way..."

I've heard about him,
of course; read his work.

This evening, our first together
as roommates, as
grad students
at a summer course
at this ancient university:
I'm speechless.

"I'll compromise," he says
studying my face.
"I'll only play it
on my side of the room. How's that?"

"Ludicrous," I mutter.

"Oh, you know the artist?
Ludacris?"

Before I answer
he's turned up the volume:

"Move bitch, get out the way
Get out the way bitch, get out the way..."

A first night's

party—red wine,
paper cups,
cheese cubes.

Max and I huddling
behind hands, speculating
on the others: "You see
him?" whispers Max. "Eyeballs
swiveling like that? Irish,
for sure. Hearing the inner voices.
Doubtless homicidal."

I, liking this game, whisper back:
"That woman: Long black
hair, lacey dress. She keeps knives
in that blouse,
I'll bet."

"Not knives," says Max. "But sharp
enough. It's Margarita.
Watch out."

And Margarita turns as if
she'd heard; strides over:
"You two: Spanish
aunts, gossiping
behind fans. Be ashamed!

Max giggles; tangos
fiendish steps.
I, reddened,
allege one strangled
"Olé!"

"This is how I get the girls," Max whispers

about to read his poetry.
"Yes," I whisper back.
"I'd like to see you do that
I really would, since Max's poetry
is sentimental horseshit
and nobody should fall for it.

Yet, when he begins to read,
I watch the girls look up with interest
at his story of brothers
in their little town—how sad when one disappears
in autumn, in the lake, under a running tide,
at sunset.

Others are taken
by his story of first love—her
parting words to him—heartbreaking and yet
with delicious, artless irony,
and hilarious because of it ...

...and so on he reads,
and on,

until, I swear, every woman in the room
is taken, and,
in truth, I may be a little taken,
myself.

When he's done, the girls collect around,
some teary eyed with wistful
smiles, but all with pens
for him to sign
the books he's thoughtfully brought
to sell. ("Always carry your books,"
he *sotto voce* instructs. "You never know when
your market will get hot.")

To each girl he whispers something,

in answer to her praise. I can't quite
make out what he says,
but he says it with sincerity.
("Oh yes," he instructs me
afterwards. "You must learn
to do
'sincere'
really, really well."

My turn upon

the stage. And I've got
something
that'll hold their attention;
like Max, something
that'll get the girls.
"This," I begin,
"is a story of the hijacking
of English poetry
in the year 1559!
Of forgery, duplicity,
prosody!"

I pause. *This
is going to be good.*

"It's 1559. Martyrs' fires burn
in England—
a time of political correctness
and innovation, as well.
Commerce with Europe
brings contact with Continental
literature—judged superior
to the home-grown kind.

"In London, printer
Richard Tottel sees a market
among the elite, educated public
for the best new poetry
England has lately produced.

The manuscripts circulating privately
in courts could rival, if printed, anything
by Italians or French, to show
foreigners England is good—
better—than them at
their own game.

"Tottel hires Nicholas Grimald,
famous Cambridge scholar
and translator. They collect,
carefully edit 271 poems,
mostly by Sir Francis Wyatt,
Henry Howard, Earl of Surrey,
Nicholas Grimald, himself,
as well by "divers
other."

"The first edition,
called *Songs and Sonnets*,
sells out in weeks.
In the next months
Tottel reprints
seven times, editing, rearranging,
getting sloppier,
each edition selling out.

"Meanwhile,
imitators abound:
*The Paradyse of Daynte Devises, A Handefull
of Pleasant Delites, Gorgious
Gallery of Gallant Inventions,
A Mirror for Magistrates...*

"*Songs and Sonnets* is famous
for one hundred years, credited
with establishing English poetry,
especially the sonnet, the primacy of the iamb,
the patent English schema. Even Shakespeare
has Bottom lament: "I had rather than forty shillings
I had my book

of *Songs and Sonnets* here."

"But there is mystery, too.
Modern scholars discover
the poems of Wyatt and Surrey
in their authors' hands
[are not the same as printed
by Tottel.]
Of Wyatt's "Satires," John Thompson
(*The Founding of English Metre*,
New York: Columbia University Press, 1966), writes:
'The Satires as printed by Tottle are not
Wyatt's Satires. The metrical principle
is quite different from Wyatt's; the true difference
cannot be tabulated statistically.'
A.K Foxwell (*The Poems of Sir Thomas Wiat*,
London: Russel and Russel, 1964) takes it further:

'I went to the MSS. in 1906, and compared the variants with those in the author's
own text... Wiat's individual characteristics were obliterated... It is evident, then, that
Tottel... adopted a style of verse *contrary to Wiat's method....*'

"Why?" I ask rhetorically.
And I answer
in Foxwell's words:
"'...to suit the views of a later
generation.'"

I pause, having
made my point. But Max
demands:

"So what? So what does this prove? So what if this printer fellow cleans up
primitive verse, yielding us great poetry, glory of English Lit.! What's wrong with
that?"

"That's all true," I blurt.
"But here's another way
to see: Would English poetry
have evolved in unexpected ways,

with more likeness
to its forbears—yes, Chaucer
and Langland, and even
Beowulf—poetry
more akin to the Beowulf poet shouting:
"Hwaeth! Listen up!" to his cyn—
a community event—something
for "the people," not only "the public"
(as Tottel defines),
if Grimald and friends
kept greedy hands
off genuine
merchandise?"

"I don't believe it," says Max.

"Don't you see?"
        I plead,
"Don't you see that Tottel snatched
real English poetry, replacing
it with counterfeit?
Verse that sounds like nothing
anyone ever
spontaneously said?"

Silence.

I try again:
"All this time
we've seen it one way: the glorious
increase of poetry
over four hundred years."
        (I begin to gesture
        compulsively.)
"But, if you have it
the other way,
what we've got is tragedy,
forgery!"

Silence.

What I really want to do
is leap about furiously,
like the obsessed grad student I am,
to scream:
Tottel and his henchmen must be arrested!
Must be taken to the place of darkness
to be hanged until
they are dead!
But there are limits,
and so retreat myself
into silence.

The session over,
I'm the only one left.

Later, alone with Max

I try again:

"I wanted to read a poem
that I would understand. Though
I hated them all:

"Among the worst
the pedestrian Longfellow:
Evangeline drilled by rote in school,
> (Though the 'Druids of eld, with voices sad and prophetic,'
> standing 'like harpers hoar, with beards that rest on their bosoms'
> amused sixth graders.)

"Or murderous *Invictus*
> ('Out of the night that covers me,
> Black as the Pit from pole to pole,
> I thank whatever gods may be
> For my unconquerable soul.')
Also by rote.

"And then grim Victorian tabloid poetry:
> ('Oh, Heaven! It was a frightful and pitiful sight to see

Seven bodies charred of the Jarvis family;
And Mrs. Jarvis was found with her child, and both carbonized,
And as the searchers gazed thereon they were surprised.')

"And the magnificently flatulent
'Ode on the Mammoth Cheese, Weighing over 7,000 pounds':
('We have seen thee, queen of cheese,
Lying quietly at your ease,
Gently fanned by evening breeze,
Thy fair form no flies dare seize.'

Why was I the only one laughing?)"

"Ho hum," yawns Max.

"And worst of all, twisting
plainspoken psalm
into tortured syntax,
        (i.e. 'The Lord to me a shepherd is
        Want therefore shall not I.')

"Are you telling me
these bastardized things
are great English poems?"

"No," I retort. "But they
are the children of Tottel,
bastards nonetheless,
and we must vouchsafe
them our attention,
or what's
an English department
for?

"In any case, these things pained me."

"I can see how they would," says Max.

"Pained me,
until a friend showed me
something."

"Did he, indeed?" arched brow Max.
"Was it Wordsworth:
          ('Give me your tool, to him I said.')
It wasn't Wordsworth, was it?"

I sputtering:
"I meant, a poem
he'd written himself,
in a language we spoke,
and not in artificial
mouthfuls that no one
ever
spontaneously
said.
And about
important things..."

"Ah," says Max. "And what meaning
did this poem hold
for you?"

I looked up,
anywhere for the words:
"...That it was modern English,
unadorned
with obvious figures.
Yet it was to my hearing...something...
something..."

"Yes," says Max quietly. "Magic."

He understands at last, I think.
But then:

"I understand your
argument,
but cannot believe
it."

"We'll put on a talent show,"

Max announces. It's
nearly end of summer
and school.

"Don't worry," Max reassures.
"I'll arrange it all."

He sets about
recruiting class clown,
Dickie Needles, who,
known to Max only,
plays classical violin.

"When you come on,"
Max instructs,
"wear this old bathrobe.
Everyone'll think you're clowning.
Then give'em Brahms."

Max conscripts Argol, silent
the whole term, author
of a so-far incomprehensible
dissertation: *Otiose Warts.*
He's discovered
Argol can recite
from memory
the complete dialogue
from *The Towering Inferno.*
The catch is: Argol
won't introduce scenes, won't
change voice for
different characters speak;
simply recites

and recites

until stopped.

Next Max reels in
Yuki, who owns
a kimono and
a *koto*, six feet long
that she offers to play.

Then steely Margarita.
Large, muscular, she
announces she'll perform
graceful interpretive dances
to Yuki's playing.

"Well, she plays piano, too." Max
confides, almost an apology.
"I'll have her do
something with me
at the end."

"And what is it
you're planning to do
at the end?" I ask.

Max mysteriously, "Perhaps
I'll sing a little."

(And
I can already hear it
in my head
"Move bitch, get
out the way
Get out the way bitch, get out the way..."

That'll give the audience
something to think about, I warrant.)

Comes show night:
wine jugs, cheese cubes
paper cups.
Everyone's pleased, eating,
drinking.

Max appears. Theatrical
bow. "Ladies and gentlemen
let us begin."

Dickie Needles,
nervous, bathrobe
flapping, arms
akimbo. We
giggle at the clowning
sure to come.
Out flourishes the violin
and his serious
music, so unexpected,
mesmerizing.

Genuine applause
when Dickie's done.

Next comes Argol.
Who is this
anonymous man?
Argol silent, brick-like
before us,
opens mouth,
begins....
        the loudest human tone
I've ever...!
Crashing tank tread! As if
an army endlessly
invades us
in some old film loop.

Five, ten, fifteen
minutes of this.
I cut my eyes
and catch Max's
sadistic smirk.

Finally, Max
breaks in; shoos

Argol.

Then it's time for Max.
The audience may
be confused. But I
can't wait
for Max
to ruin himself.

But he doesn't.

Margarita at the keyboard
of the old baby grand.
Max sprawling across
its top, crossed legs. Quietly,
as if the cafeteria lights
had gone down, as if candles
were playing, he tells us:

"My mother
always wanted to sing.
She dreamed
of performing in nightclubs,
with big bands. But
she stayed home, raising us kids.
Even so, when Dad worked
the late shift, she would
sing to us."

On cue, Margarita begins
to play.

"I'm going to sing
my mother's songs."

In naive, untrained voice—
not tenor, nor baritone—
somewhere out of spectrum,
Max begins "The
Man I Love."

Some day he'll come along, the man
I love./ And he'll be big and strong, the man I
love...

He charms us, damn it.
Damn nit. Charms us
from the start! It's a torch song.
Max pretends
no skill, doesn't clown.
It's his vulnerable voice, childlike,
forever trusting mother,
that of a little boy three or
forty years old.

What can we do but cheer?
We're all happily
drunk, so what the hell..

Before his
final song, some of us begin
to weep.

I begin to weep.

("It's all timing," Max
confides later. "A fart
is high art
when you cut it right.")

I'm back

in the stacks,
worrying Tottle's
in my teeth
like a dog.

Why won't Max
believe?

"You've got to make

the case
for forgery, if that's
what you allege."

"And how am I
supposed to do
that?"

"Motive," declares Max.
"Find the motive
for it."

Start, then, with Tottel, the man:

"Richard Tottel (or Tothill)," writes Hyder Edward Rollins (*Tottel's Miscellany*.
Cambridge: Harvard University Press, 1966,) born at Exeter about 1530... printer of
distinction...charter member of the Stationer's Company (under-warden in 1561)—
blahdy-blahdy-blahdy—began about 1550, at the sign of The Hand and the Star in
Fleet Street. Prints law books, mostly, Greek and Roman translations. Some minor
poetry: Tusser's rhymes on husbandry and "huswifry," the works of Sir Thomas More.
Oh here: Cicero's *De Officiis* translated by Nicholas Grimald, who later turns up as
chief editor of the *Miscellany*.

I read on
and on,

still no motive
for forgery. But
I'm after
this dude, Grimald.

Here's a mystery:

Forty poems of Grimald printed in the first edition of Tottel's. Eight weeks later,
surpassing success, with Grimald responsible, and a second edition appears, sells
out immediately. Yet, inside, only nine Grimald poems remain, and Grimald's name
excised altogether. Why this messing with patent success? Why this alteration?

"Today the name of Nicholas Grimald is almost unknown," writes L. R. Merrill (*The
Life and Poems of Nicholas Grimald*. New Haven: Yale University Press, 1925) Yet, his

contemporaries regard him as foremost Cambridge alumnus, great English scholar, playwright, translator, teacher, preacher (chaplain to martyred Bishop Ridley) and so on. "One wonders why it is," asks Merrill, "that a man so highly rated is now quite forgotten?"

Interesting Grimald:

His father a promoter—that is, an extorter of money from the wealthy on behalf of the king. (Executed for this by a later king, although a devoted husband and kind father, according to Grimald.) At Christ Church Grimald sees published his play, *Christus Redivivus—The Resurrection of Christ*—performed. And many times later, often in Germany, used as original text of Oberammergau's anti-Semitic Passion play, held every ten years in thanksgiving for deliverance from the Black Death. He translates Cicero's *Octavium de Republica,* Virgil's *Georgics*, and more. Then, interestingly, experiments with poetry in English applying Greek metrics, dactylic hexameter. Much technical success, to be sure, but unpleasant to the ear.

But he persists, eventually bringing the poems of Wyatt and Surrey to Tottel. Perhaps he models his own verse on Wyatt's, though we know he rewrites his betters, and, as *coup-de-maître*, awards himself the lion's share of Tottel's pages.

There is also unsavory Grimald:

Ecclesiastical timeserver, shifting from Catholic to Protestant in the political wind, recanting secretly, betraying friends, "as," writes Merrill, "was necessary to save his life." His friends, hanged or burned—his, hardly the life of pure scholarship, though not unknown to the English department. The Bodleian Library holds a poem of Duke Humphrey's, Grimald's contemporary, a *Carmen in Laudem Grimmoaldi,* a song of praise, which concludes: "Since you do all things with a desire for transitory praise,/ May the gods give you praise, but brief praise, O Grimald."

Grimald rewrites the poetry in Tottel's, but why? To suit the taste of the day? No, because his rewriting establishes that taste, in the first place. Because he had studied European poetic forms, judged them superior, wished to bring them to the English line? Yes. But is it forgery?

And why do I pursue this
doggedly? I ask
at day's end, at the end
of the day

I must be insane.

This is it

a blank night,
a break
before nervous
sessions commence,
defending our theses.

Max, heady
with triumph, announces
that tonight, in the rec. room,
he'll invent
for our amusement
the *Café Casablanca*.
"I'll find tablecloths. We'll
have menus. We'll serve
coffee, tea, wine. Pastry!
A real boulevard cafe!"

Everyone's thrilled,
of course. Me too. I want to help.

Max is harsh: "Why
do you always want to collaborate?
This is my party. I'm not going to let you
take credit. You're the competition,
don't you know that?"

Rejected and flattered,
both at once.

Eight-thirty that night:
I walk my date,
Yuki
down the dorm stairs.
Max at the door,
suit and tie,
hair neat. "Welcome," he,
unctuous, greets us.

"Shall I show you
our best table for two?"

The room dusky,
flickering candles.
brutal cinder block decorated
with streamers. Each rickety table
disguised with gift paper.
"Your server," he says
"will be with you shortly."
Max is our smiling,
gracious host.

The party under way,
we are loud, celebratory,
dancing to the boom-box
Max has found.

Then, at midnight
I see Max alone,
sipping wine. "Congratulations,"
I tell him. "You've got everyone
playing a part
in your fantasy cafe."

Max, annoyed, dismissive
says, "It needs only a good idea to get them started. These people love to role-play.
That's what they've been doing since they got here: playing the serious student role.
Now, I've given them something else to play at. They're very happy."

"Aren't you unfair?.
It's not play-acting. After all,
we *are* students."

Max looks at me now:
"Don't you see? It's a cover. Half these people came looking for a man, for a woman,
for validation of their lives from people superior to themselves.

"What role am I playing, then?"

A pause. "You pretend," he says "to be the young apprentice. That learning for the sake of learning is a sacred, mystical quest. You act woolly-headed, confused, but you know more than you let on. You're really watching everything with a sober eye. And you're angry with me right now because I've unmasked you!"

Well, I was angry. So what?
But unmasked? I don't think so.
I do hold learning
for its own sake
noble.

"Have it your way," shrugs Max. "You're deluding yourself, just like the other creeps. You think you're knights on a holy crusade. Actually, you're only the Don Quixote-types, inflating ego-needs with fantasy. You think it's the Moors attacking across the Spanish plains, but it's just a flock of sheep. That's why you all walk around bumping into each other. Your eyes are on the prize, but the prize is a mirage!"

Furious now, because I love this graduate study, my fellow students, I recall the scene in Don Quixote wherein the innkeeper invites the insane old man to stay so he can laugh at him and have his guests laugh at him.

I remind Max of this.

"Yes," he says, "I remember."

Then, finally triumphant, I want to know:
"Why is it you innkeepers, you reality-grounded cafe owners, why is it you get so much pleasure from torturing us poor lunatics?"

Max is stunned, but only
a moment. And I'm gratified.
He slaps tabletop with palm. "Bravo!"
he laughs. "Touché! You got me!
I didn't think
you had it in you!"

I, relieved, flushed with gratitude,
take the hand he's offered. My anger
fizzled, he's
conceded the point.

I accept
his validation.

"I can help you," says Max.

We're allowed one
peer on our dissertation
panel. Now on equal footing, I
invite Max onto
mine.

"I'll coach you, get
your act into shape."

We review everything I've pursued
this summer.

Max considers:
"Maybe you've found the motivation for fraud. Grimald wants his own poems
published, but nobody likes him much. So, he does the hard work of the anthologist,
puts together something irresistible, and then gets a free ride on Wyatt's coattails.
That's his hidden agenda.

Hmm," concludes Max. "I think it will play."

I think it does,
if somewhat. Professors
quiet throughout. At the end, the
usual silence. It is the right instant
for Max to grab the moment,
to validate my work, to concentrate
the judges' minds.

Of course, Max
does seize the moment
and pronounces:
"No. No. I just don't
believe it."

And then sly

smile for me: "I," says he,
"vote it down."

Afterwards, I
ask why? Why
this betrayal?

"You're the
competition," he says.
"I already
told you that."

It seems strange," writes

Professor Thompson (op.cit.) "that Tottel's *Miscellany* should rise like a wall
separating poets in Tudor England."

For instance, Wyatt in his own hand: "It was no dreme: I lay brode waking." But then
revised by Grimald: "It was no dreame: for I lay broade awaking." A subtle change,
but the line is regularized.

It felt like no dream, in any
case. I'm walking
the Tudor alleys.
A man, hurrying,
at me, his
face in my face.
"Yo," quoth he. "Bitch.
Move."
It's Nick
Grimald—tall, thin,
eyes of a wild horse, black hair
flapping in wind.
"You got me!" he shouts.
"I didn't think
you had it in you. But
you got me."

"What?" I ask, trying
to wake up.

"But you blundered importantly.
        I didn't become master of form
to imitate lesser others.
        First my poems—unprecedented
in our language,
        and made at great expense (witness
dead friends, milord Bishop
        Ridley). Then to showcase,
I worked flawed, ratty,
        rattling-on-floppy feet
rhymes of others—reformed them,
        raised them up,
made them holy
        or wholly imitations
of my own. I say
        in all humility:
It is from me
        whence you derive
your present rhyme."

"And what of your friends,
burnt at the stake?" I ask. "What
of Saunders, martyred
at St. Albans, for preaching
against the Roman
Church? He handed you
the cup of martyrdom..."

"He asked me would I
drain it? Die with him
on the morrow?"

"You refused the cup..."

"No, I took it, as
he insisted, and drank instead
to his very good
health."

"And you were arrested, sentenced
to drawing-

and-quartering, then to
hanging..."

"They wanted
Ridley. I obliged, offering
everything I knew,
becking and bowing
my knee unto
Baal. And
I was at liberty."

He studied
my face, my accusing
eye.

"Its bastards betray
martyrs. If I'm to be
the bastard,
it's bastards that
maketh art."

So saying, pushing past me,
"Move, Bitch."

Then I lay broade awaking.

from *Forty-Nine Guaranteed Ways to Escape Death* (2007)

FROM THE CATALOG OF PROHIBITED MUSICAL INSTRUMENTS

for Ariana (a.k.a. Chloe)

I. The Octuba

The conductor
of a symphony orchestra
built the *Octuba,*
after his own design.
A weird musical instrument
it requires eight strong men
and women to play it.
Its music
is *basso profundo in extremes,*
and its vibrations
dislodge bricks
in adjacent buildings.
People in the streets
fear earthquake.

It is rarely played,
and remains illegal
in twenty states
and the District of Columbia.

II. The Novelty Concert Piano

Edward Clement, Inventor: "Back in the ` 20s we made a special piano for orchestras
touring the hinterlands. This piano had a lot of built in extras to amuse the hicks. It
could chirp like a bird, croak like a frog, or boom like a thunderclap. It could laugh
and shriek in a hilarious human voice, cluck like a chicken, howl like a dog in heat, or
even produce water closet noises.

"By mistake we shipped one to Carnegie Hall."

"Paderoosky played it with the Symphony. Midway through the *Requiem*, he discovered the special controls and had great fun cranking them up all at once for a riotous climax."

"I understand the audience loved it, but Carnegie Hall complained, so my employer threw me out, along with my piano."

"They don't make pianos like that now, and I think you'll agree these techniques of piano manufacture are better forgotten."

III. The Tandem Flute

Two musicians,
who face each other
and blow
into each end,
play the silver
Tandem Flute.
The instrument,
only a half-meter
in length,
is capable of making
delightful music,
but the players
themselves
are often uncomfortable
staring into each other's
eyes
at short range.
This has led to violence.
In 1876,
the acknowledged masters
of the instrument,
Phil Wundt and Harvey Fechner,
settled a long standing
disagreement
when Wundt blew
a poisoned dart
through the barrel of the flute,
killing Fechner.

Following this,
as a matter of law,
hooded or blind
performers only may
play the instrument.

IV. The Musical Scaffold

Before inventing
the electric chair
Thomas Edison

proposed
a moral cautionary
for mass executions:
the condemned
would be hanged
from ropes
braided of metal
instead of hemp.
Each would be tuned

to a different
note, and,
as bodies

dropped through
trapdoors
in sequence,
a solemn musical
composition
would sound.

If
hanging a party
of four,

the ropes would play
the portentous
opening notes

of Beethoven's
Fifth
Symphony.

If
a party of eleven,

the ropes could
be tuned
to play
"Fear not
my friends,
for the worst
is yet to come."

As an economical
alternative,
Edison proposed

that criminals
be hanged
from church bells,

their bodies, descending
and ascending
as the bells swung,
ringing

the musical
changes.

As Edison
was mostly deaf,
it is improbable
that he
had any serious
understanding
of music,
anyway.

V. The Multiple-Percussive Timpani

As Pyotr
Illyich
Tchaikovsky featured
live cannon fire
in his *1812 Overture* Op. 49,
so the anonymous, hooded composer
of the *Falluja Suite*
has given contemporary realism
to his composition
by including a deadly modification
of the orchestral Tympani.

In this composer's plan,
remotely controlled units
are hidden in secret locations
of the audience.
When activated these instruments
produce the sounds
and shock waves
of actual roadside bombs.

The composer has instructed
that the audience,
including those with heart conditions,
not be informed
about the presence of his *Multiple-Percussive Timpani*
so that the performance
may be climaxed
with authentic
"collateral damage."

Insignificant Meetings
with Remarkable Men

"The un-readiness is all." —*attr. G. I. Gurdjieff*
for Denise Duhamel

1. My father knew General Eisenhower. I was three or four. He took me to meet the ex-president during half time at a Colgate vs. Army football game. "How are you, my boy?" Eisenhower asked, patting my head. "I have to wee-wee," I supposedly answered. He bent down and supposedly confided, "I do, too."

2. On Fifth Avenue, on the way to the "Merry Mailman" kiddies television program, waiting to cross the street with my father, I pulled the gun out of a big cop's holster. The cop whipped around while my father stood back. "Gimme that, you little bastard!" I was upset that the cop had shouted, and so probably cried.

3. The Great Someone-Or-Other (a once-famous magician reduced to performing at children's parties) tried to amaze us with a trick in which you drop shredded newspaper into a cake pan, light it, then cover it, say the magic words and a real cake appears. I was smarter, though. I had my own magic kit. I rushed to the stage and unmasked the cake pan's false bottom. I received no applause, and the magician looked sad.

4. The principal of my progressive school had a persistent fascination with Alain, a classmate from Haiti. "It's the chicken guts," Alain told me. "Everyone in my family tells the future by chicken guts." According to Alain, the principal would call him from his classes and they would meet under the apple tree, where the principal would question Alain about the divination of the stars and the planets. Alain asserted: "He believes everything I tell him." The principal was a stern disciplinarian and nobody's fool. But years later I heard he'd been fired, losing the school's money in inexplicable transactions. Reportedly, he pinned the blame on his personal oracle.

5. The summer before I was sent to military school my father introduced me to an older boy who attended there. Grown up, the boy is now a well-known real estate tycoon, owner of gambling casinos, and a famously angry star of his own TV show. At school, he was always nice to me, though he never laughed at my jokes.

6. Our military school chaplain was a war hero, credited with killing many men, though a priest. One afternoon, he caught me under the library smoking cigarettes. He ordered me to his office, reappearing in military uniform. I expected a tongue-lashing. Instead, he marched me to the commandant's office, whining: "This boy! A member of my religious instruction class!" The commandant awarded me one hundred punishment tours to be marched in dress uniform, a big M-1 rifle on my shoulder. I never respected the chaplain after that. He used to close his sermons with quaint New England expressions, such as "Keep your peckers up, boys." He'd seem bewildered when we'd laugh at him, gleefully taking his good wishes the wrong way.

7. At fourteen, the books of the English humorist, P.G. Wodehouse entranced me. On a family trip to England after my father's death, I had hoped to meet the famous writer. But a publisher friend of the family told me that Wodehouse hadn't lived in England for years. In fact, he was living in America, only thirty minutes from my own town! Back in the States, I looked up his address and wrote to him. He answered in one line, "Sorry. I never knew your father."

8. I attended college in the Hamptons, home of many painters. The Abstract Expressionist, Willem de Kooning taught elementary painting. "It's lonely in the winters," de Kooning told me. "It was either teach with your friends in the daytime or get drunk with them at night, and end up in jail." Once, at his studio on an errand. I'd brought my girlfriend. De Kooning offered me a tall glass of Scotch. Then on the wagon, he insisted on watching me drink. When I'd finished, he chased my girlfriend around the studio. As soon as I could, I begged her to leave with me. We left, despite his offer to show us his latest paintings.

9. With Chiara, the ten-year-old daughter of a friend living in Venice, I crossed the bridge to Ezra Pound's home. Chiara and Pound played chess now and then. Pound and Olga Rudge, met us at the door. Though supposedly in his silent period, Pound was full of conversation. "We play all the time. She always beats me," he told me. "But do you play?" I told him I didn't. Silent then, he turned and headed for the chess table. Olga Rudge made me a cup of Lapsang Souchong tea. "He loves his game," she told me. Crossing the bridge on the way home, I asked Chiara how it had gone. "Beat him, as usual," she answered.

10. A year later I returned to Venice. The last boat for Il Cemetario was leaving and I'd just had time to catch it. Pound had died, and was buried near the graves of other idols: Igor Stravinsky and Serge Diaghilev. I'd only begun to search for them when, behind me, a bell pealed. I turned and saw the great wooden doors of

the cemetery closing. I escaped but had seen nothing I'd come to see.

11. As a student at Columbia, I was given plum assignments, escorting visiting writers around the campus. I met Jorge Luis Borges, the blind aristocrat poet, at his subway stop, and offered my help. His translator and aide, Norman Thomas di Giovanni answered for him: "Thanks, but we can find our own way. After all, I went to school here." Later, I was asked to help the famous poet and communist, Pablo Neruda, to the airport. "No need," his driver told me. "He'll take his limousine."

12. "One knew other poets when one was at university," W. H. Auden told us on a visit to our classroom. "But one would never expect to find them in such an odd thing as a Creative Writing class." Auden was wearing blue jeans, a plaid shirt, a pair of bedroom slippers and (I imagine but am not sure) sipping a Martini. He proceeded to denigrate all poetry except traditional meter as a means for teaching students. He offered to help us learn the classical forms. I don't know how many students returned for his next class. Being a modernist, I didn't go.

13. At the Cathedral of St. John the Divine, they were dedicating the Poet's Corner. Later, Robert Penn Warren stopped me in the street. He'd been a guest of honor at the ceremony, but now wanted directions to the subway. I did my best to be detailed and exact. After all, he was an old man and might get lost. I even offered to ride with him to his destination. When I'd finished my detailed instructions he replied: "No, I think I'll take a cab."

14. Jean Erdman, wife of Joseph Campbell, had produced a play by a friend of mine. At the reception held at their apartment, I ran into Campbell on the balcony, gazing at the twilight sky. What a wonderful chance; however, I'd read none of his books. "Nice evening," he observed with his familiar lisp. I agreed that it was, indeed, a nice evening. He turned and walked back inside.

15. Years after I'd been his student, I became a teaching colleague of the only poet on the English department faculty. We had been good friends, but he'd betrayed me. "How many poets do you think *can* be on an English department faculty?" he asked after he'd blocked my tenure. I was angry, plotting revenge. Not till years later did I see a chance for it. My enemy had become deformed with Parkinson's, his arms festooned with bandages. "It's the drugs," he complained. "When I dream, I act out. Last night I punched my fist through the window." Now, in my triumph, I felt nothing but pity—no pleasure at all.

16. I published a long poem about a writer I'd known in graduate school, a terrific manipulator. Thoroughly self-centered but brilliant, he often disparaged my projects, claiming that I shouldn't be surprised as I was "the competition." At a book fair, years later, where my new book was on display, I was staggered when he appeared in person, walking down the aisle. He had aged, but over the years had gained national fame and respect from readers and other writers. I was sitting behind the counter, watching him approach. Without noticing me, he examined my book in familiar head-tilted, birdlike posture. I was thrilled that he might buy my book! I imagined his surprise when he'd begin the poem and instantly recognize himself! He stared for a time at the book cover, but walked away without saying anything.

17. Trying on a leather jacket, I commented to the clerk that a few silver studs would make it look really cool. "The stud," replied the clerk, "is inside the jacket." As I admired myself in the mirror I noticed that I was taller, leaner, sexier—dangerous looking. What a revelation! This was the real me: a remarkable man! I imagined a new life of wild successes, overmastering men, seducing women. However, the jacket turned out to be too expensive, so I bought a different one.

I Channel Truman Capote

The Petulance of the Deceased:

Well, let me see....
Do you have any peanut butter?
I think I might like to spread some
on a cracker.
My, you seem to have
a large collection of bric-a-brac.
Nick-a-nac.
Is there a theme here?
Or is it all random stuff
you found in the street?
I like this one especially:
the plastic palm tree
with the sign
"Welcome to Brooklyn."

What kind of host are you?
Standing all-agog.
If you're expecting me to say something witty
then you've picked the wrong moment.
It's certainly dusty in here.
I think I'd like a glass of something.

The Omniscience of the Deceased:

The winning number is 3741823.

Put your money on Lubricious Sister in the 8th race at Santa Anita.

Just use some lemon juice.
The stain will come right out.

No. She doesn't love you anymore. Doesn't even

think of you.

How tedious you are.

The Moral Righteousness of the Deceased:

Yes. I did visit the house in Sagaponack on New Year's Eve. There were boys I knew living there. I was disappointed when you answered the door. I was in a funk and sat down on the couch and didn't stir for hours while you and the boys reveled at some poor poet's party. And during that time I absolutely did not do the nasty things you claim in that defamatory—if happily unpublished—essay.

But, meanwhile, you got ripping drunk and spun your car on the ice, nearly killing everyone. Nauseating, your behavior, really. I recommend you throw away that essay, in which you pretend to be the hero, and print this one, instead.

A RARE VISIT TO MY FATHER'S OFFICE

I don't think I'd ever seen him in action, giving a presentation to colleagues. Later, I sat close by. He really was a handsome man, but with a dueling scar that I didn't remember.

"What I wanted was to be articulate, to be on a stage addressing millions," he lamented. "But you see how I've tied my fingers in knots? Unlike your generation, we rarely had a public forum."

True. We, living, hog the spotlight, our authorized biographies in every stupid song, our faces on every milk carton, our full names in answer to any question you care to ask.

Still it was nice to see Dad, one grownup to another. Now he was articulate about his shyness, his ambivalence about having once been alive.

THE SHOP NEXT DOOR

First it was a shoe shop.
        The shoemaker so poor,
he slept on the floor
        and resoled customer's shoes
with cardboard.

        ✈

When it was a clothing store
        the young owner
decorated her window
        with grace and invention,
one spring hanging a sign
        "Just Married!"
and posing manikins
        as bride and groom
holding pictures
        of her own wedding.
Another spring
        her sign read:
"It's a boy!" and she dressed
        her manikins
in blue
        surrounding them
with toys.
        For Halloween,
she costumed the manikins
        with sinister masks.
But in December,
        when she dressed them
in Christmas finery,
        she neglected to remove
the sinister masks—
        which troubled us
as we ate our breakfast

and watched
from next door.
       Later, she hung a sign:
"Divorced. Closing Store."
       She'd stripped the window
and abandoned the manikins
       to their nakedness.
Under the stark
       neon streetlamp
they glared at us
       like Arctic snow.

✶

Now the shop
       is run by a man
selling buttons.
       He has reptilian swiveling eyes
and dresses formally,
       as if royalty,
always wearing
       a lengthy metal chain
from a window curtain
       as a watch fob
on his polka-dotted vest.

A Snowball

Ginsberg threw a snowball
at Frank O'Hara's coffin
at the bottom of its grave.

"Damn," he whispered as he threw it.
"Damn, damn."

"A lovely, sentimental story," Ginsberg told me
when I'd asked him about it.
"Improbable, however. Not true. You see,
he'd died in July.
Who told you this?"

"Schwerner, I think."

"Well, Schwerner wasn't there."

In time,
I imagine Ginsburg's grave.
Nothing sentimental about it:

the open earth

a snowball
balanced

at the edge.

Forty-Nine Guaranteed Ways
to Escape Death

1. Aunt Elizabeth didn't believe in death. "Just go up to the coffin and sprinkle water on his face. He'll wake right up. You'll see; they always do."

2. Wes, my cab-driving colleague told me that the first thing his mother invariably said upon viewing the deceased was, "My, doesn't she look healthy?"

3. Eileen Tabios' father died on April 11th, my father on April 10th, my brother on April 9th , and Burt Kimmelman's mother on April 3rd. Our calendars are filling up. Under the new rules, only one person you know is allowed to die per day. After the 365th there will be no more death.

4. Ron owned the funeral home where most of my family had been laid out. I'd begun to consider him my personal mortician. One day I met him at the bank. "I sold the business," he told me. "My friend and I were born the same day. We turned sixty. My friend dropped dead at our birthday dinner. It shocked me. I'd never really thought about death, I guess." He had to do something, he said, so he was going skiing.

5. Joseph Heller's character, Yossarian cultivated boredom to prolong his life. The actor, George Saunders' suicide note read: "I was bored."

6. In the end, Carlos Castaneda, unable to burn with "the fire from within" implored his disciples to "intend me forward. Intend me forward!" beyond death. But despite his disciple's intentions, he died. He was cremated. Later, his disciples told the world that he had not died at all. Instead, he had entered the realm of the "third attention." They continue to defend their belief against all. "Intend!" they shout at their doubters. "Intend! Intend!"

7. A lesson from Scientific American, 1980: "We used to believe in the particle theory [of light], but now we believe in the wave theory, because all who believed in the particle theory have died."

8. On Halloween night, 1982, at Sleepy Hollow cemetery in Upstate New York, two boys found a newly opened grave, tunneled to the adjacent one, opened the

coffin and propped the corpse against the tombstone. The next day, as the funeral of the husband began, relatives were amazed to discover his dead wife posed as if awaiting his arrival. "She always said she'd see the old man dead," a relative recalled. "I just didn't know how she'd pull it off."

9. From an Internet story: "Yes, I realized, my patented Acme Hero Anti-Death Suit had saved my life yet again."

10. Bessie the Cow, our childhood pet, her brass bell clanging merrily as she moos: Moo, moo. No dear, we don't eat the cow. We eat the beef, the boeuf, the steak, the fatted calf. No, not the calf. We eat the veal. And not the bah, bah lamb but the mutton. And not the bunny but the lapin, the hare, the game. We hunt, and it's not only for the eating but also for the immortality to be found in transubstantiation of fish into seafood, pig into pork, and deer into venison. But when there's no game afoot, when there's famine in the land, then there remains only Bessie the Cow. How do we separate Bessie from the children, and the children from the starkness of the moment? We take the merry bell from Bessie's neck, lead her to the barn, and send the children home. "Cheeseburgers for dinner!" we promise.

11. Fred told his friend he napped eight times a day and enjoyed a long night's sleep, as well. "Why waste your life that way?" asked his friend. "There'll be plenty of time to sleep when you're dead." "Ah," answered Fred. "But when I'm dead there will no longer be time to dream."

12. When my friends and I were young we watched horror flicks on midnight TV. *Dracula, Frankenstein, The Wolfman* and *The Mummy*. From these we learned that to cheat death one must become a stalking, devouring monster. On the third day, when the rock was rolled from Jesus' grave, his friends must have been terrified.

13. When George's father died he complained to a religious friend that, no matter how much he had prayed, his father had not come back from the dead, as Jesus had promised. "You have only to wait for the right time. It could be one year, or one thousand years. Just wait." George's heart was uplifted. "Thanks," he told his friend. "I didn't know you could do that. I'll just sit right here until it happens."

14. Houdini visited the graves of family members and magicians constantly, examined the long-dead bodies of his father and brother when they were reburied, and once traveled out of his way to see the burned bodies from a

schoolhouse fire. As someone remarked: "For a man who had resurrected himself so many times, how strong a barrier could death be?"

15. Don't bury your old loves. They'll drag you into the ground with them. If you can't let them drift up into the sky, at least run with them through the forest of your longing.

16. "The earth is suffocating," wrote Frederic Chopin at the end, in 1849. He begged his friends to have his chest cut open so that he wouldn't be buried alive.

17. A method to avoid live burial, 1850: A pull cord is built into the coffin. It runs to the top of the grave and thence to a bell. Should the occupant awake after burial he need only pull continuously on the cord to ring the bell, which will serve as an alarm. The caretaker, should there be one present, will hear the bell and then re-open the grave, releasing its occupant."

18. When all seems lost, write a letter to your departed loved one and pay to have it printed on the obituary page. Apparently, the deceased read obituary pages, judging by how many letters to them are printed. Now the problem is to figure out which newspapers your own departed ones read.

19. "They sell charms here that ward off death," said Katya, my Grecian beauty. She told me they are blue with an eye painted on to deflect death. You wear them on a necklace or a bracelet. According to Katya, the poet Homer is said to have worn one on his forehead and warned his enemies: "I may be blind but I've got my eye on you!" She said you could also purchase a blue bead to wear instead of an eye. Blue is the color that wards off the death-stare, but it is also commonly thought that blue-eyed people are exceptional givers of it. "So beware when a blue-eyed person pays you a compliment, it could be your last," she warned. (However, modern science has proved that death can result from the actions of people of other eye colors, as well. —ed.)

20. Grandfather cautioned: "Don't grow old!" I promised I wouldn't.

21. [Illegal immortality scheme redacted.]

22. We took a high school art trip to the Guggenheim Museum. They were showing the French Impressionists. At the top of the long spiral gallery was a painting by Van Gogh, "Starry Night." A man glared at me. He leaned over and hissed, "I'm standing right here so you better not make fun of my painting!" I didn't realize

until later that if he really was Van Gogh he must have been well over 150 years old. Also, he'd grown his ear back.

23. Two Recipes: For Death, construct an effigy of yourself. Go to the cemetery and get some dirt. Try to do this during a waning moon, when the moon is in Scorpio or Capricorn. Construct a small box. Light a black candle. Put the effigy into the box. Bury it in the graveyard. Do not think about the spell as this will interfere with its working. For Life, reverse these instructions.

24. Do not open this door. Do not open that door. Do not open the door over here, or the door over there. Or the inside door. Or the outside door. Neither the porch door, nor the front door. Neither the closet door, nor the refrigerator door. You don't need to know what's behind Door Number One, or Door Number Two, or Door Number Three. Don't open the door marked "Private." Don't open the door marked "Come In." Don't open the trap door. Don't open the fire door. Don't open the coffin door.

25. Do not live at home. Most fatalities occur in the home.

26. Make your last day at least 25 hours long.

27. Be too goddamn mean to die.

28. My children (if I had any) tug at my shirtsleeve. "Daddy," they beg. "Please don't die." Although I do not have children, I promise them anyway: "I won't die. I'll stay alive. For you."

29. Make a list like this, but don't stop.

A Ten Thousand Dollar Bill

A woman asked if I could change
a ten thousand dollar bill.
I told her, "Nobody can change
a ten thousand dollar bill."
But I opened my wallet anyway
and found that I had ten
one thousand dollar bills.
"It's your lucky day!" I told her.
"Here's your change."
She gave me a wink
and a big smile.

Later that day
another woman asked me for change
of a ten thousand dollar bill.
I told her, "Nobody can change
a ten thousand dollar bill."
"But I just saw you change one this morning," she argued.
"Won't you open your wallet again and look?"
So, I opened my wallet,
and, yes, there was change
for a ten thousand dollar bill.
"It's your lucky day!" I told her.
"Here's your change."
However, counting it out
I noticed that the first ten thousand dollar bill
wasn't in my wallet. I'd never taken it
from the first woman!

I ran back to the first woman,
who was still smiling and winking,
"I've spent it all," she said
in answer to my question.
And now tears filled her eyes.
I felt sorry for her

and opened my wallet
to give her the second
ten thousand dollar bill.
But my wallet was empty!
I quickly realized
I'd never put the second
ten thousand bill in my wallet!

I ran back to where the second woman stood.
"I've spent it all," she told me
tears filling her eyes.
I patted her hand.
All I could do was stand there
holding her hand.

Eventually, I found
comfort for myself:
Even if I'd had
the ten thousand dollar bill,
it wouldn't have done me any good,

because nobody can change
a ten thousand dollar bill.

THEIR GOD

One afternoon, their God announced that he would destroy the world. (Someone had made a silly joke about him and he'd taken umbrage.) "I could wipe you off the planet with my snotty hankie, or burn you with my cigar," he thundered. "Instead, to teach you a lesson, I'll do it in a way you'll understand." As part of our punishment he announced that he would build an explosive device of incomprehensible destructive power. Then the sky roiled with red and blue lights and swirling clouds. From out of the sea, his splendid figure arose, magnificently muscled, standing almost seven feet tall, and wearing a peek-a-boo loincloth.

Then he walked upon the land. We heard that he'd set up shop in an old barn. Someone saw him at the dump, scavenging parts from discarded televisions. He even came to our door looking to borrow a screwdriver. A month later, the rumor was that he'd taken a job pumping gas in order to pay the rent on a larger workshop. We trembled at the thought of his huge bomb nearing completion and of the horrendous consequences to follow. We'd already packed our bags, withdrawn our savings from the bank, and let the cat out.

Months passed without cataclysm. The newspaper reported that he had made a speech at a Rotary Club dinner, and the mayor had suggested that he might do well in politics, perhaps becoming a judge. The big factory he'd built at the edge of town for his bomb construction was the second largest employer in the county, surpassed only by Wal-Mart. He was becoming a community big shot, always smiling and throwing kisses when you'd meet him in the street. It was rumored that the leading political party wanted to draft him for the mayor's job. Anyone could see that he was enjoying himself. Gradually, we began to relax, tentatively unpacking our bags.

But still the threat of imminent annihilation was there like an annoying insect, buzzing and biting when you'd least expected it. We didn't know whether to renew our magazine subscriptions or pay the cable bill. "Why torture us this way?" I asked my wife when the newspaper hinted that he might be secretly dating a movie star. "Why doesn't he just get it over with?" My wife mused, "There's something about these immortal beings," she said. "They're thinking, 'Screw 'em! We've got all the goddamn time in the world.'"

MY FAVORITE TV SHOW OF ALL TIME

for Achilles and Gabriela

A beautiful collie watches me from the other side of the TV screen.

You could look into her eyes and imagine all sorts of adventures:

> *the time she saved the boy from the abandoned well;*
> *the time she saved the boy from the abandoned mineshaft.*

You could look deeper and find something wordless, ancient:

the Ur dog. What company sponsored that show?

All I know is that my friends and I gnawed on dog bones for years.

Now, Mother tells me she has to go out.

"Don't leave the room," she warns.

"If you do, that big dog will get angry."

I look at the dog: she's seemingly asleep.

Gathering my courage, I stand up.

But the dog is instantly up, too, growling, barking, clawing the
screen, and showing fearsome teeth.

Terrified, I sit down. After a moment, the dog sits.

Soon she is yawning, her eyes closing.

But it is enough: I know now that she will always be watching
me, throughout my life, even in reruns.

GOOD WISHES

for Barbara

I felt her hands on my face.
It was the middle of the night.
"You're burning up," she said.
"Would you like a cold towel
for your sunburn?"
"Thanks," I told her.
"But you don't have to get up."
"It's no trouble," she answered.
"I've just got one for myself. See?"
I looked over
but saw no towel anywhere.
"I'll get one for you, too,
they're so refreshing," she sighed.
Then she rolled over
and began to snore.

How the Work Gets Done

I challenge my dream: "Show me the Equator. I've never seen the Equator." And I'm there, registering at a hotel on some tropical island in the middle of the ocean. I look around expecting the exotic but everything looks depressingly ordinary, as if this were some grubby convenience store in Canarsie. "Show me things I've never seen," I command my dream. I'm imagining succulent equatorial flowers; blossoms billowing like parachutes, and juicy fuchsia-hued fruits big as boulders.

The scene changes, but instead of embroidered nature, I find myself in the hotel's unremarkable cocktail lounge. Some guests have dressed formally. Others are naked. We're just a bunch of people sipping our drinks, probably waiting for dinner. We attempt conversation, but it goes nowhere. "This is nothing," I scold my dream. "Show me the horrors, the spectacular horrors of the Equator!" I'm imagining spiders towering like skyscrapers on stick legs, and malevolent vampire insects numerous and unremitting.

Nothing outwardly changes, although, one by one, I begin to recognize my fellow guests. In fact, I know every one of them and I wouldn't voluntarily spend a second in their company! I notice, too, that everyone now is looking around the room and recognizing everyone else. From their gloom I surmise that everybody has discovered mutual hatred.

Can it be that, compelled by the rules of civility, we must spend our short, once-in-a-lifetime equatorial vacations in this Sartrean hellhole in intimate contact with those who revolt us? But then it dawns on me: "Thank you," I tell my dream sarcastically. "For showing me this true horror of the Equator!

At the Funeral Home Bar

This funeral home is impressive, shiny new, vast as a convention hall, coffins and mourners everywhere crowding the horizon. Over there, the dancing Hassidim; yonder, the phlegmatic Peloponnesians. Every religion, every class is accommodated. But I'm here on business. I roll my mother's wheelchair toward a couple of idle morticians. "Could you watch her for a moment?" I ask. "I've got to meet someone at the bar." "Certainly," they answer. I can tell they're about to give me that creepy mortician smile that says: *You don't know what we know about what happens next.* However, I don't have time to humor them. I've got business at the funeral home bar—

— which turns out to be a lovely place, warmly lit and crowded with genuine, friendly folk. No rude barroom jocularity here. Indeed, they make quiet, respectful jokes. Occasionally one will place a comforting hand on another's shoulder.

I've come here to meet my friend, but time passes and she never shows up. "Your friend is late? Get it? She's your *late* friend?" says the gentleman next to me. I laugh politely. "Don't worry," he says. "Sooner or later she'll show up. They always do."

But she doesn't, so I decide to head home. Once off the barstool and onto the floor, I realize that everyone here is extremely tall. Even I seem to be taller than when I came in. "Mourning will do that to you," says the gentleman next to me. "Sadness does it. Let me show you," and he makes a sweeping gesture with his hand. The scene is transformed. We're no longer affable people at a funeral home bar but tall pine trees in a forest. It is winter. The air is clear, cold. And though we stand together, each of us is somber and alone.

Escape from the Fat Farm

DAY 1: "Cappy", our dining room host, announces: "You'll be served delightful low-calorie meals, and you *shall* lose weight!"

DAY 2: I gaze at my plate. The solitary pea that was on the edge has rolled over the rim and disappeared.

DAY 3: Cappy says beware the alligators in the moat. And keep hands off the rabbits. Delectable, yet their bites are deadly.

DAY 4: The table talk has turned entirely to food—if at breakfast, then about lunch. If at lunch, then about dinner. Then breakfast again. We are insatiable in our talk about food!

DAY 5: We suspect Little Tubby Moran has caught and eaten a rabbit. Our jealousy knows no bounds.

DAY 6: We've been debating the best method for capturing an alligator. "Can you whistle and they come?" No. "Can you call them: 'Hey, alligator! Hey, alligator!'" No. "And would pan roasting be easier, or stuff it whole into the oven?" Probably neither. "I'd rather have the shoes, belts and handbags," observes adorable Penelope, but the rest of us know the truth. She'd wrestle an alligator to death, its fritters steaming in the sun, if they'd just let us out of this building.

DAY 7: Our conversations are now whispered because Cappy is watching and listening, his hands clanking metal ball bearings, like Captain Queeg. He is definitely suspicious of our whispering.

DAY 8: The meals get no better. A slight diversion: our waiter, a new daddy, shows off his infant child. This event leaves us quiet, meditative. Our tablemate, Dr. X, an admitted amateur torturer, opines that cleaning, cooking and eating a human infant is as simple as cooking a baby pig. We find this horrible and disgusting, and we tell him so. But this leads to speculation on where we might find a baby pig.

DAY 9: Cappy now appears each night dressed as a pirate, complete with wooden leg. He twirls his pirate's gun and reminds us by certain gestures that it's loaded.

DAY 10: Someone serves us the wrong dinner! The menu said Steak with Mashed Potatoes and a Chocolate Milkshake! But all we got was a plate of spoons! Not even a steak knife! Little Tubby Moran complains loudly, but answer gets he none.

DAY 11: We are served a bowl of murky soup made with moat water. An openly hostile Cappy commands: "Get in there with your spoons and row, you blackguards!" And he fires a warning shot across our bow. It is understood that we must now address him as "Captain."

DAY 12: Little Tubby Moran has disappeared. Nobody says it, but we're all thinking the same thing: *cannibalism.* Dr. X is missing, also.

DAY 13: There is open talk of mutiny. The captain has chained us to the deck. We're fed only low-fat yogurt with the occasional strawberry floating in it. But all we need is the opportunity and Cappy goes down. Then we'll row ourselves across the moat to freedom and a good brunch.

DAY 14: A terrible storm at sea. Cartons of croutons and little packets of mayonnaise float by, but always out of reach. Penelope says: "Let's see if we can swim as far as the kitchen. I'll get a decent meal if I have to kill someone!" We manage this, and are awed. Refrigerators, their shelves weighed down with food, loom. And there is something else. In the blackness a lone figures stands between us and our dinner. It is Cappy aiming his pistol. "I'll take care of this," Penelope hisses, darkly determined. "This night we eat!"

DAY 15: Morning sun and quiet sea. At last, it's all over. Cappy has vanished. The dining room doors have opened. We, tattered survivors, pull ourselves together. Outdoors, a bucolic scene: alligators dozing like armored cars on the moat banks; sounds of tiny sprockets turning inside the bodies of caterpillars. And as we're led to the scales, we discover to our delight that we have lost weight, exactly as advertised in their brochure, though it's mostly arms and legs.

FROM THREE URGENT REVIEWS

Argol Karvarkian, *Otiose Warts*. (Bergen: Univ. of University Press. 2006)

This forty-fifth collection continues Karvarkian's obsession with miniature poetics: lyrics gorgeously wrought, each with the grace and identicalness of a Faberge egg. It is curious that after Karvarkian's decades of writing and publishing well-mannered volumes, his many readers may not recall his earliest work, which is characterized by a surprisingly primitive, even brutish sensibility. A far cry from the lapidary incrustations of his contemporary work, his earlier poems seem to have originated in a swamp: metaphors dense as quagmire, often expressed in grunts, such as "Bleep. Fsssssh. Poof." Contrast this with the minimalist clarity and grace of a lyrical refrain from a poem in his newest collection: "This. That. This."

I first met Karvarkian in Florida. I had recently married, and my wife and I shared a shack on stilts in an obscure part of the Everglades, where I could work on my literary criticism in solitude. Karvarkian was young, of course, with massive, unkempt hair and musky odor. The three of us became friends after we'd met at the local fishing-themed bar in town. Gradually, I began to notice the attraction Karvarkian and my wife shared, and so I wasn't surprised when one day he took me aside and growled, "I'm leaving on a lengthy journey to reach the end of the world. And, oh yes, do you mind if I take your wife?" He was surprised, I surmise, by my gracious accession.

There then seemed to be an endless supply of wives in the Everglades, so I had no trouble marrying again. What did astound me, however, was that within a month of my second marriage Karvarkian reappeared, his long trip apparently cut short. He pointed his finger at my trembling first wife. "I don't like this one," he told me. "But your new one seems entirely lovable. Do you mind if I take her along on my infinite journey?" Naturally, I greatly protested. Wasn't one enough for him? But my new wife flashed her eyes and I obliged her.

This left me in rather an awkward position. My first wife and I were no longer properly married, but she didn't seem to be leaving the house, so we resumed our cohabitation with the proviso that I might at any time, should I wish to, take a new wife. Eventually I did.

It was then that Karvarkian once again reentered our lives. "Take this one back," he ordered, thrusting my second wife at me. "Lemme have the new one." Numbed, I could only allow her to go.

Now I was living with two former wives. After some time, I remarried. Moments after that ceremony, as if he'd been lurking beneath a trap door, Karvarkian abruptly appeared demanding the new wife in trade for the old.

This pattern continued for some years. Eventually I stopped protesting because I'd begun to notice that after each exchange of wives a new book of Karvarkian's poetry would appear. Each time, I would read it with immense interest and greatly marvel at his progression of intellect and technique from volume to volume.

His eighteenth collection, *Phlogiston, You Bet*, evidences what we might call the typical Karvarkian poem of the early middle period: distinctive language and budding obsession with the mysterious shadow figure, eventually to be known as the Procurer, so famously developed in later volumes:

*A can of f*****g beer*
*collides with a f*****g cold thought:*
Pimp me vittles,
*that little b******d*
better deliver
*me f*****g flame-retardant*
flapdoodle another beer
*in f*****g skirts*
*or I crush his f*****g*
smooch. ("A Bone Aren't Made of Beer")

By his thirtieth volume, *We'll Burn That Bridge Before We Invent It,* his outlandish verbosity has given way to a diction both natural and unforced:

The notion of amber gosling
waddling, My sainted Procurer
in his red wheelbarrow.
"Ducky," I coo. "Get me another
in her flowing skirts. This one's gone dry."
Gosling nestles, but tiresome Procurer
demands recompense.
Grudgingly,

I flip him the bird. ("The Pushover Prize")

Although I support forty-six ex-wives on the meager receipts of my modest critical efforts, I can't help but believe that I had something to do with the great Karvarkian's evolution as a poet. After all, he seemed to extract a tangible grace from the women I married—and, I flatter myself—possibly because of my own connection to them. I'd also like to think that my judicially crafted critical prose, which my wives have assured me they read aloud to him each evening, helps to discipline his earlier poetic unruliness.

I can think of no better evidence of this than this latest volume. Here he demonstrates, with a directness characteristic of his formative earlier work, what may be a final, summative reconciling with the Procurer, the mysterious shadow-figure:

Needles, needles.
Glockenspiel headstrong.
Ale may ail and skirt hurt,
but o my sissy-brother,
there is nary the consumer
absent the consumed. ("Elapsed Bumbershoot")

Whether this mysterious Procurer will ever be brought fully from the shadows must wait on future Karvarkian collections, although significant criticism has already appeared. (See my *The Mysterious Procurer in the Poetry of Karvarkian.* Three volumes. Freemont: Univ. of University Press. 2004)

Still, if we are to consider the totality of Argol Karvarkian's oeuvre, we must ask, what does it signify? What will be its influence? These beautiful Faberge egg-like poems, several dozen to a package: how are we to understand such exigent fragility? I think, in the end, they will share the fate of all delicately created things. Like Faberge eggs they will abide as objects that we can admire, but that, once having admired, we relegate to the collector's shelf without further comment.

Sandy's Mother Reviews *The After-Death History of My Mother,* by Sandy McIntosh (East Rockaway: Marsh Hawk Press 2005)

He was always a disappointment. He should have run a bank, but he barely passed math. He should have been a wealthy lawyer, but he leaves his fly open and stutters in public. Look how he misinterprets my good intentions when I find these nudie pictures in his room:

✖

My mother had rummaged through my room, never saying a word, leaving the naked
pictures there for me to know she knew I had them. I was never beyond her grasp.
Private parts would never be private. She herself was a greater force of nature than even
adulthood, and we both knew her name was Silence. ("Private")

Well, boo-hoo. I like things to be in order. How did I know how ungrateful he'd
be each time he came home and discovered I'd rearranged and repainted his room?
These were acts of love! Then he goes about copying down my senile remarks as if
they were just the cutest things! For instance:

The hospital parking lot is empty.
My mother's in her favorite chair refusing to speak.
"Such a character," laughs her roommate.
"She touches you and tells you you are healed
and may go home."
Her roommate hands me a pamphlet
with favorite quotations of my mother
assembled by the other patients:
a collection of libelous rumors concerning my wife and me.
One passage, supposedly from Jesus, reads:
> No one knows what will happen
> when I leave my tomb in the night
> to touch you. ("The Hospital Chair")

He's nothing but a plagiarist, a poseur.

In another poem he has me sleeping in the snow after I supposedly wander away
from an Alzheimer's institution. I was never in an Alzheimer's institution! And I've
never slept in the snow! Then he says he dumps me in the Public Library where they
videotape me each week until:

... I was told that the library's funds had run out
and my mother's project would be terminated.
I would never see my mother again,
since over time she had become an image on a screen,
and the library would pull the plug. ("The After-Death History of My Mother")

Well, in his favor, he does get something right:

We lower my brother's coffin
beneath his monument.
Abruptly, mother hisses: "Look!"
Not twenty feet away,
another monument,
the grave of my brother's nanny.
"She wanted him for her own," mother whispers.
"Now she's got him."

A decade passes.
The game of Cemetery Chess progresses slowly.
Mother dies; her monument
erected midway between brother and nanny.
As we lower my mother down
I whisper to the nanny: "Check."

It's justice that we keep the old bitch at bay. Still, I resent him using me, prying open my coffin, looking around inside, touching things, moving them. It's a cheap way of making a buck. Even this book review I'm supposedly writing strains credulity.

Remember that film, *Psycho*? Well, that's him, my son. He's put on his mother's dress and he stabs at me with that horrible knife!

from *Ernesta, In the Style of the Flamenco*
(2010)

ERNESTA, IN THE STYLE OF THE FLAMENCO

in memory of Frank Wolfarth Walsh

Music will watch us drown. —James Tate, "Read the Great Poets"

[The stage: Ernesta, in disheveled Flamenco costume, sits on a stool before a
battered upright piano. A banner overhead reads: "Señora Ernesta, Pianist, Gives
a Recital in Aeolian Hall—reviewed in *The New York Times*, February 21, 1927."
Throughout the monologue, Ernesta's hands often seem about to touch the piano
keys to illustrate something, but she pulls them back hesitantly without playing,
until the penultimate scene.]

[Entrada Libre]

1.

¡Ay!
That old bastard Leschetitzky,
To whom I was sent to study in 1885
Pushed me out disdainfully
(After I'd rejected him) onto
Clara Wieck, relic of the dead composer,
Robert Schumann,
At Frankfurt am Main,
And mistress (I didn't know at the time)
Of that fellow Brahms.

She was, I thought,
Not a bad pianist,
And she performed for me
The last sonata of Beethoven.

Superlative, the music. Like you,
I was moved to weeping.
But she took my tears
For love of her

And left the bench
To mount my lap.

"I knew you had a soul," she declared.
"I knew I could inspire it."
Saying which, she began to rub
My costume.

What could I do? I was sixteen—your age,
She perhaps forty—altogether ancient
And unattractive, you'll agree.
But it is our duty to realize our talents.
And so, I yielded to her pleasure
With enthusiasm, and at length.

[Caña]

2.

"You must wear your costume
    On stage, at receptions," Wieck instructed,
        Directing my career.
"The music can never be enough
    For the bored husband in attendance,
        Or the jaded wife. You must distract them
From the incomprehensible,
    Let them pass the time
        Avec plaisir."

She was here
    Referring to my costume—
        A Flamenco dancer's,
Something my mother had sent
    From home—I could not imagine why.

"It's a handy prop," Wieck explained.
    "The vest with satin and gold ruffles—
        So heroic—
And the revealing trousers, also,
    So feminine."
        ¡Ay! ¡Ay! ¡Ay!

3.

So, onto the stage she thrust me,
  Arranging concerts
    In little theaters in great cities,
Always in the shadow of her true lover,
  The bumptious Brahms.
We were oddly twined, Brahms and I.
    He overwhelming the *Grosser Musikvereinssaal* in Vienna
     While I, the plodding dray-horse,
Through *Malagueñas, Granáinas, Media Granáinas,*
  And other tedious transcriptions
    Of Spanish dance music

For the Ladies' Tea Society,
  Or some such,
    Located somewhere
     Near the wharf.

In his splendid dressing rooms
  Brahms received the King and Queen.
    I, in my turn,
Attended the
  the Ladies in Waiting,
    Waiting for me,
In my backstage
  Hole in the wall.

"You are, after all, the beginner.
  There is a price to pay for advancement.
    Pay it, grin and be happy," ordered Wieck.
     ¡Ay! ¡Ay! ¡Ay!

[Alegrías]

4.

It was, I must say, a lovely,
Lucrative time. Lachrymose, the
Germans for music, crying at
Each arabesque, every waltz, the

Ushers running the aisles with lace
Handkerchiefs for the ladies. They
Cried in the streets for a popu-
lar tune. And, God help us, When a

Fashionable composer died!
Old Glück's funeral—four months long!
Multitudes of musicians in
His memory. Accompanists
to the country's wistful, obliv-
ious   dreaming   .

[Cante Libre]

5.

And I also dreamed deeply
On my concert stage,
Fascinated spectator
To imaginative scenes unfolding
In my mind as I played:
Elaborated image upon image.
And, over years,
My visions joined by dream actors
Who never failed to amuse.
I never asked, "Where am I?"
So certain was I of my strengths.

Old Beethoven in his time
Laughed at his audience
As, by mere whim,
He played to make them weep,
or whimpering silent—
Or, who knows? Feint dead away.

I, too, made listeners quake,
But I loved them (unlike him)
And only wanted them
To witness what I saw—
Those ecstatic things.

And, naturally,
They did see,
And honored me
With applause
Joyful noise,
Duly noted by
Music critics.
"Señora Ernesta Pleases."
¡Ay! ¡Ay! ¡Ay!

6.

I pleased them—
I pleased myself—
In every European country,
Yet Wieck kept me
In Flamenco costume,
And touring everywhere but Spain
(Where they preferred
German pianists
In lugubrious
lederhosen).

All went well.
I played a wider repertoire
Dropping stale Spanish ditties
For music of weight,
Of darker dreaming,
Yet always pleasing my audience,
With novelties
As *finale*.
My special piano
Made by mad
Clement of New York.
At my whim it would
Chirp like a bird, croak like a frog,
Boom like a thunderclap, howl
Like a dog in heat, shriek
Like a parrot, or
Emit rude sounds of
The water closet.

But then
(It was somewhere eastward, I think,
In the Ottoman Empire),
Something went wrong,
On stage, playing dream music
The audience with me
(I could hear them swaying,
Moaning
In their seats),
As I brought the music
To its graceful end,
(So I thought,)
I found myself
Not at the piano,
But in the wings,
In my street costume
About to leave the theatre.
What had happened?

"You walked out before finishing, Mademoiselle,"
Said the stage manager,
Perplexed.
The audience behind us
Restive, uncertain.

7.

What had happened?
I'd been playing
Robert Schumann's "The Poet Speaks",
Its lovely grace, its sadness.
I alone on the empty stage,
In dreaming. As usual,
The music done, I bowed,
Retired in modest dignity,
A caress to the souls
Of each listener.
But this night
I had not
Awoken from the dream.
(That must be the answer, I surmised.

I'd remained in the music
Even leaving the stage
And almost into the street.)

Next night:
Again it happened.
Am I mad?

I consulted Wieck.
She looked at me sadly,
Concerned.

"This is what happened to Robert,"
Her husband, the dead Schumann.
"He wandering away
into his dream,
never to return."

(I'd heard Schumann had died in Bedlam.)

"It's a conceit, affectation, indulgence
To pretend music has pictures,
Has a story to tell.
Robert knew, in truth,
That music is only music,
Though that knowledge
Gained him nothing."

For my part,
I had no idea what she meant.
Music, of course, had stories
And pictures, to pull
Us away
From quotidian quarrelsomeness,
Waking-life vexation.

"Music," she continued,
"Is a wild beast.
She must be
controlled,

caged
Else she turn upon you
Destroying all."

Unbelieving, I
Shook my head
Not speaking.

"You need to see.
I'll show you," she declared,
And took me
To Byreuth, to vulgar Wagner's operas,
Der Ring des Nibelungen.

The horror of them!
¡Ay! ¡Ay! ¡Ay!
Through their music
I saw what Wagner saw:
Shades of the monumental:
Males and females towering above mountains,
Lumbering over the earth,
Lathering bloody ancient ritual,
Never intended for
Modern times.

"To loosen grasping grip
On him, Robert
recklessly wrote
Music without program,
Without picture,
But picaresque withal, you see,
And touching, too:
'The Poet Speaks'
His first attempt.
To break the curse—no pictures
At all! Or so he thought.

"It turned out
To be the worse for him,
Losing his way to the music's end

Without the markers, the maps.
The pictures.
And, at last,
He was lost.
Alack."

Lest I, too, lose my way,
She told me
I must avoid all music with programs,
With stories, damn pictures
Able to lead me to
Unknowable dungeons
Of darkness in dream.

8.

Fear and caution
Gathered me in,
Nourishing my performance
With hungry diet
Of the safe
And acceptable
"You cannot afford," said Wieck,
"To disgrace yourself upon the stage.
Not even once!"

So, it was back to the safety
Of *Malagueñas, Grana'nas, Media Grana'na,*
And other tedious transcriptions
Of Spanish dance music.

Twice I attempted to break free,
Challenging the forbidden
"The Poet Speaks,"
The first time with mild success,
But the second
With terror,
Finding myself in the stalls,
Applauding wildly,
While the audience stared
At the empty stage.

From then, I resolved to ply
The narrow road
Without imagination.

9.

I was already forty
And should have been
At my zenith.
But still I performed
In Flamenco costume,
Though certain sure
I'd outgrown it
Long before.

Humiliation shared residency
With any triumph
I achieved.

10.

Worse,
My modest sensation and fame
Had competitors.
Two especially (I won't mention names)
Attempted to crowd me
From the stage.
One toured with burros
That wandered about
Diverting audience attention.
Another boasted
Masked dancers
In silent pantomime.
Both, of course,
Imitated my costume,
But elaborated
Upon it:
One by smoldering phosphorous flairs,
The other by transportable
Electric lights.

11.

They were nothing,
No threat to me,
Like the real threat
Of Enrique
Granados.

He, a likeable man,
A genuine Spaniard,
Wore no special costume
When performing—instead
In mufti—and playing
His own compositions,
Originals,
That left the sting of lemon
On your tongue,
And the red Sahara dust
Of the *leveche*
On your tongue,
And the yawning
In coolness
Of the afternoon veranda.
Tropical is what he was,
And boon
To frigid European winter.

He was my enemy,
Though I liked him
Well enough,
And sympathized silently
His suffering
Hallucinations
And terrible stage fright.
I offered my council,
Telling him: "Don't worry.
Just go out there. You'll think
Of something."
And, against my true hope,

He did, always.

I copied his improvisations,
Claiming them for my own.
(I, by then,
So frightened
By imagination's wildness
That I could do
Little else.)

He, in turn,
Loved me,
Questioning me about life
And travel—something he feared
Greatly.
Then (it was 1913 or 1914)
His *Goyescas* found
International success,
And he received an invitation
From America,
To concertize
For the President.

Impossibly nervous,
He asked would I go with him,
Discretely, of course?
He had certain nightmares
While playing his piano....
He'd pay my way
I to stay with him
For companionship,
No personal intrigue,
Help him
Understand the New World.
He'd pay my way.

12.

He'd pay my way.
It would be the retainer

And the retained.
But, why not?

I could see very well
The end of Germany,
The sentimental music
Fueling visions
Of majestic ascendancy.
Germany
Apex of Europe—
Her composers
Told her so.

Why not go with the boy?
But his dreadful foreshadowing:
"I play my music
And dream of the ship
Torpedoed," he confessed.
"The seawater
In my nose,
Choking me, filling
My lungs.
I know this to be
Hallucination,
But come with me.
At least keep my mind
From the bottom
Of the sea."

Hallucinations
They were,
So much like my own,
But, for him,
Not far off the mark:

The warring powers
With deadly sea weapons:
Sinking ships.
Our daily news.

[Caña]

13.

Consulted I with Clara Wieck.
    She (one hundred years old
        If a day by now)
Was doyenne of composers,
    Beloved of the powerful.
    She advised:
"Go. There is nothing
    For you here."

She arranged passage
    From France
        On the *Mirabelle*,
A Spanish freighter.
    "My friends inform me
        That Spanish ships
May pass our blockade
    Unharmed. It is
        The English ships
            That must capsize."

At the dock
    Granados waited
        Nervous, pacing.

'So glad to see you!'
    Clutching the hem of my *mantón*.
        "I thought you would never come.
The most awful dream!
    I dreamed it
        Last afternoon
At the salon
    At which I played."

"Ah," I tried to reassure him.
    "It was only a dream.
        Music does that
            To us all.

"*Mirabelle* is
     A solid ship. A Spanish ship.
       We will feel
         At home."

"The dream so vivid!"
     Stammered he. "The ocean
       Broke through the walls!
I, swept away!
     Then you,
       Sitting in a lifeboat.
You waved your fan. 'Bon voyage!'
     Paddling away."

He began to cry;
     I patted his shoulder.

The *Mirabelle* sounded
     Her great horn. Granados
       Refused to board.
"I cannot travel
     On this ship,"
       Declared he
         With finality.

I reasoned:
     "All our luggage—your beautiful piano
       All are aboard!"

"No, no. You sail."
     His eyes lolling.
       "I'll take the next ship.
Which one? Ah!
     The *Exeter* sails Friday.
       I'll take the *Exeter*,
         A good British ship."

"No!" I cried,
     But he not listening.
       I could have told him

British ships
  Would be torpedoed.
    But, no. I did not.
A terrible sin of omission?
  Or was it the tact
    Of a lady?

"Next Wednesday," said he
  With wild grin.
    "We meet in New York
      Next Wednesday!"

14.

Arrived in New York,
  The news report said
    The *Exeter* had been sunk
Only a few miles
  From Le Havre.
    Survivors,
      There were none.

[Desplante]

15.

In short,
Granados dead,
I was offered
His place, playing
For the American president
As I had suspected
I might.
I had taken the precaution
Of registering
In my own name
All his original compositions,
His wonderful piano! Its
Rosewood cover!

And so I became established
Unchallenged, respected

The greatest interpreter
Of the works
Of Enrique Granados
(Which I, at times
Of convenience to me,
Called my own
Compositions).

16.

For several years, at least
My longevity in the public eye,
Enhanced via
Old Leschetitzky,
Who, now arrived in New York,
A sentimental place
In his halting heart,
Coaxed me to play
For the mechanical piano
Granados' music,
To make piano rolls
For the wide appreciation
Of music-loving
But illiterate
Public.

Thus when nightmares on stage
Returned,
(Young Granados
In the sea, willing water
To solidify for handhold,
Failing, drowning,)
I could tease tunes
Safely
From the player piano
With pumping pedestrian feet,
Staying trembling,
Haunted hands.

17.

When I play
For my public now
I play for safety—no silly
Pictures in my head
To preoccupy me,
Only the plodding
Scales, chords, the arpeggios
Of the novice—
At adventurous times,
The exercises of Hannon,
And Clementi—
That in lesser hands
Might seem ridiculous,
Elementary. But genius
Will out!

[Ernesta strikes the keys violently playing a scale, arpeggio, or other elementary piano exercise as if performing the climatic movement of a masterpiece.]

And I am never reckless!
My arms and torso
I do not wave about
Like a *puto*!
No more
Wild musical
dreams!
¡Ay! ¡Ay! Ay!

And after my concerts
I read the newspaper
And it is always:
"Señora Ernesta Pleases."

[Soleá]

18.

Don't look   shaken, *chico*.
She is a wild animal,   this music,
She must be   controlled,

Caged   else she turn upon you
Destroying all.
Arrogant armies   stamping feet across
Continents   Inspired, each one,
By some   affected anthem
Dribbling sentiment,   some musical monstrosity
Imaginary righteousness.   What better exemplar
Of menace   and disgrace?

If I may present you a proverb
Of my own invention:
"Music ," I will caution you.
"Music will watch us drown."
¡Ay! ¡Ay! Ay!

(I applaud myself: *¡Olé!*)

Minute Mysteries:
The New Adventures of
Inspector Shmegegi and Monica

1.

I awoke. Monica was waiting. "I need to borrow your car to drive 1,000 miles. I could be back in a couple hours."

Some quick calculating. "One thousand miles in a couple hours?" screamed I, incredulous. "That's a 2,000 mile round trip! It would take at least three hours!"

I was new in town and driving a rental. I didn't want to run up the mileage.

Monica's tears fell on the sodden sheets. "But I ironed your clothes—and your wallet." She pointed to the dining table, where I could see everything from my wallet (even the secret things from the hidden compartment) neatly unfolded and pressed.

I was thrilled, but mostly alarmed. "Look," said I. "I'll give you a ride to the edge of town. That's the best I can do."

She sat in the backseat. We drove, crossing a puddle in the road.

But it wasn't a puddle. It was a bottomless lake!

The car sank. I got out the window but Monica was locked inside. "I'll save you," I shouted, but all that came out of my mouth were bubbles.

Frantically I searched for the key. It was a big key chain and I wasn't sure which one would open the door. Then I remembered: it was the safety deposit box key!

But by then I'd run out of air and had to swim to the surface.

Help Inspector Shmegegi solve the case. Answer these questions:

1. *What were the "secret things" Monica found in his wallet?*
2. *Why would only the safety deposit box key open the car door?*
3. *Do you think Inspector Shmegegi secretly felt safer with Monica inside the car?*

2.

I was fascinated by Monica's body jewelry, embracing and mouthing her every diamond and sapphire. Then the door flew open. It was the Insane Man with a machine gun. "I am the real Inspector Shmegegi!" he screamed and began firing. But no one was hurt; the bullets were blanks!

I contemplated the Insane Man and remembered him as some beachcomber who'd drifted into our home one afternoon many years ago. He was harmless, though given to unpredictable bursts of rage. He was living somewhere in the attic, I recalled.

Help Inspector Shmegegi solve the case. Answer these questions:

1. *Why did the Insane Man burst with rage?*
2. *Why was the Insane Man firing blanks? Was that a comment on Shmegegi's and Monica's ardent sexual forays that had yet to produce even a single hamster or bunny?*
3. *Who was the Insane Man? Was he the real Inspector Shmegegi, as he claimed?*

3.

At a big dinner party in a foreign country, I noticed Monica couldn't get the table manners and customs right. For example, between the fish and meat courses she belted out a Purcell voluntary on her trombone. Between the salad and dessert course she encouraged everyone to sing *"Deutschland über alles."*

Our hostess—a proper lady in a pearl necklace—ended the meal abruptly. "Perhaps," she told us sadly, "you'll come back some other time." (*When you've got some manners,* I hissed at Monica's ear.)

Help Inspector Shmegegi solve the case. Answer these questions:

1. *Why was Monica trying to embarrass Shmegegi?*
2. *Why didn't Shmegegi tell us about his own bad manners—for instance, encouraging his dog to pull up a chair and help himself to whatever he wanted?*
3. *Was the hostess a real person or only a fearful representation of Shmegegi's mother?*

4.

Monica had hardly finished her star turn as *"Monica, Il Volcano di Piacere"* when the stage manager threw us out to the curb, Monica in her black boots, fishnet stockings and leather whip, I in my modest tweeds, a peephole pinned to my lapel.

"How can he do it?" lamented she. "Calling me pathetically reclusive? After all, having sex on stage five times per night for more than ten years should qualify me for brighter assessment!"

This was a low point for us. I'd have to get a job. I thought hard, then an insight: "It's because of your father! Behind his gunman's bravado he was shy—too shy ever to get to know his own daughter well enough."

Monica sat with furrowed brow. "I've never thought of him like that," said she. "But I suppose you're correct. I can never be anything but my father's daughter. I should go live in a convent!"

And to my horror, she straightaway did so, leaving me behind, spending her days weaving lachrymose hankies for the broken-hearted.

Much later, with bitter irony, I realized that I'd made an error. It was not her father I'd been thinking about, but the father of some vague acquaintance, a hermetic lepidopterist.

In fact, I knew nothing about Monica's father.

Help Inspector Shmegegi solve the case. Answer these questions:

1. *Why did Shmegegi make such a tragic error, confusing Monica's father with someone else?*
2. *Does a "convent" serve the same function as a "safety deposit box," such as the one mentioned in Minute Mystery 1?*
3. *Are we getting the sense that "containing" Monica is the subtext of Shmegegi's list of Things-To-Do?*

5.

Monica rode her bicycle all the way from the Antipodes. Every twenty miles or so she'd call to let me know she was coming closer. "I love you, Shmegegi," she'd always end her phone calls. Why was I so frightened? What would I do when she finally arrived? Maybe conveniently not be home? "Oh, sorry," I would say. "I had to go away on business. I'll be back in a decade, more or less." But then I would worry she'd leave before I returned. What is this with me? Why do I have nightmares that Monica's entire purpose is to lock me away? Why do I find myself wishing the same thing on her again and again?

Help Inspector Shmegegi solve the case. Answer these questions:

1. *Is Shmegegi beginning to ask himself the essential questions that you and I have already posed?*
2. *Is it the truth that Shmegegi suffers from a defect of character from some incestuous childhood maternal encounter that makes all male-female relationships baffling and terrifying?*
3. *Is Shmegegi really the putz that we've come to believe he is?*

Shmegegi: Hey! Wait a damn minute!

Q. I'm sorry?

Shmegegi: You're supposed to help me solve the case, not pass judgment on my character.

Q. Perhaps it's a mystery of character that you've been trying to solve all along?

Shmegegi: And without much solid help so far, I can tell you.

6.

While waiting for the Great Eclipse—Saturn approaching so close to Earth that it blocks our moon—we were screening *Un Chien Andalou*, the scene in which the cloud cuts through the moon just as a man with a straight razor slits a woman's eyeball. I glanced at Monica and surprised her staring at me, as if she were enjoying the thought of taking a straight razor to my eyeball. Just then the Insane Man leapt to his feet from beneath my shadow where he had been hiding, and shouted at Monica the long list of her unacceptable behaviors he had prepared. Meanwhile, I strolled to the veranda to watch the planets slip away. It was like being on one immense cruise ship as another cut across its path, and on both ships the passengers are shouting and waving at each other happily as they pass.

Help Inspector Shmegegi solve the case. Answer these questions:

1. *Is Monica's supposed hostility toward Shmegegi only his paranoid fantasy?*
2. *Is Monica such a threat that he needs her to disfigure him or herself in order to relieve Shmegegi of his anxiety?*
3. *Are there unasked questions about Monica's feelings toward Shmegegi that we must now consider?*

7.

On the way to meet Monica at the bank, I caught sight of the Insane Man careening through the streets. I floored it, screeching off, all tires aflame, my nemesis slashing through opposing traffic. I followed, scorning danger. At last, I thought, I'm going to solve the case!

But then I must have passed out. I awoke, Monica shaking me, the car nowhere in sight.

"What did you do with my car?" demanded she.

I hesitated, struggling to remember. "I believe I sold it to the Insane Man. His car must have broken down and he needed a replacement. But see here," said I, showing what I held in my hand. "He's paid handsomely for it."

"That's nothing but a handful of beans!" shouted she.

"But," stuttered I. "They must be Magic Beans! Valuable Magic Beans!"

"Come on, Shmegegi," sighed she. "Let's get you home. This case is closed, as of now!

WOMAN IN THE BAR

My wife and I took our seats at the bar in Penn Station,
Forty minutes to wait before our train.
The middle-aged woman sitting next to me,
Wearing a frilly prom dress,
A fancy cocktail untouched
Before her,
Leaned over and whispered:
"Hello, sailor. Do you think
You're man enough
To rock my world?"
I hesitated. "I doubt it," I told her.

She turned away
And began whispering to the man
To her left. Their conversation
Intense, but every
Once in awhile she'd turn to me
With the whispered
Play-by-play: "He's got
A wife in Copaigue, but thinks
Maybe he can catch the later train
If we head over to the
Hotel across the street
For a quick one."

But by the time she'd turned back
To him, the man had stood up
Red-faced
And was rushing out of the bar.

Silence. The three of us
Alone. Then two women
Entered, and our new friend
Called: "Hey Ladies. Can I

Buy you a drink?"
But the ladies scuttled
Into the shadows.
"They probably think
I'm into pussy," the woman confided.
"Well, I can accommodate."

It was time for our train, so Barbara and I
Stood up. I turned to say
Goodbye.

"Going so soon?" she asked,
Then sighed. "Oh well.
It's been
A slow evening."

Sid and Linda Were Fooling Around

Sid and Linda were fooling around, and one day Linda told Sid she was pregnant. "You'll marry me, of course."

He thought about it. "On one condition: You have to lose forty pounds. Then I'll marry you." Sid didn't want to be seen with some drooping petunia.

Sid was an accountant and Linda a Poli-Sci major, prim and proper. They moved in together and had the baby. "Now you must begin your diet," commanded Sid.

Some days all she had was a cup of tea. Others, she stared at an empty cup. Eventually, the weight came off. Sid was amazed; Linda had become a beautiful, sexy woman.

Other men noticed. A strip club owner offered an enormous sum if she'd dance for his customers.

Linda danced. She lost more weight. The men at the club went wild when she shimmied down the fire pole in the middle of the stage.

Sid was jealous. He wanted this beautiful woman for himself. "I'll marry you now," he declared. "Let's go tie the knot!"

"Screw you, Sid," Linda answered. "I don't want to be seen with some boring accountant.

Sid drove away bitter. He'd done so much for her, he reminded himself. Got her to lose all that weight, after all.

At Le Côte Basque

She was not literary and didn't get my references to Truman Capote's tell-all about the Ladies Who Lunch.

I'd worn my new suit tailor-made for the occasion, admiring myself in the mirror as I tied my tie, as I straightened my trouser creases, as I combed my hair in supposed "Literary" fashion.

The Maître d' welcomed us as if we were old friends. I laid it on thick, pretending I knew the famous people who dined there. Our waiter translated the menu ("I've never heard of any of these dishes," she whispered. "Do people really eat snails?")

I offered to order for her. I thought she'd enjoy the Sweetbreads a la Financiere but she gagged when I told her what I'd done.

I thought a few more drinks might help, but later, she disappeared into the Ladies Room.

The main courses were cleared—replaced by dessert, by her uneaten; she had not returned.

The Maître d' invited me to a little table they'd set up for me by the Ladies Room. "We must have your regular table for other customers."

I drank demitasse after demitasse by the Ladies' Room door. At midnight the Cloak Room lady reported: "She's passed out on the floor."

I dithered, not knowing what to do. The Maître d' decided: "I'll get the kitchen staff to carry her out the back way."

Next morning she told me to serve her breakfast in bed. She was ill, she pleaded, with a tummy ache and a headache, and needed caring for.

She was not the sophisticate I'd wanted her to be! I screamed: "Make your own damn breakfast!"

"You don't know me," her eyes clear, her voice strong. "I'm not your damn mirror!"

ON MEETING JOHN CAGE

I'd been moving from scene to scene in my nightly pageant when I came upon a friend at the piano talking to a stranger. "I'd like you to meet John Cage."

Cage smiled, not intimidated by my appearance: buck naked except each foot and hand plunged into a box of facial tissues (props from a previous scene).
Cage was inside the piano stuffing objects between the strings—thumbtacks, bits of wood, a tiny bust of the Emperor Lucretin. "You see," he told me. "There isn't such a thing as a random number generator. It's only an algorithm that pretends to be random. In fact, there is only cause and effect."

Then we were silent, bereft of polite conversation.

The audience shuffled, coughed nervously. A siren intruded from the street. My friend twiddled his fingers. Then I realized Cage was performing his infamous work, 4' 33" in which a pianist sits for four minutes and thirty-three seconds in absolute silence without touching the keys.

Growing apprehension: Some people, struggling for non-chalance, displayed uncontrollable, grotesque facial ticks. Others rolled their eyes luridly, watching the big clock in the auditorium, which was telling us not even one minute had passed. I, too, was becoming uncomfortable and ashamed of my nakedness, like Adam expelled from Eden.

Anything could happen now, anything at all: Awful silence weighing on the grand piano, maybe all at once collapsing it through the stage floor, a wild whirlwind following, sucking us all down.

ON MEETING OUR DOUBLES

I had known Laurel and Hardy as young men, the skinny one always getting the fat one into trouble. I witnessed their hilarious attempts at building a house, the hapless brick and mortar structure about to crash down around them. I walked away watching Stan contemplating a daffodil, sweetly distracted from impending doom, and Ollie just about to scoff, "Well! That's another fine mess...."

Hours later, I stopped to watch two other men at work. Though older than Stan and Ollie by thirty, forty or fifty years, they looked remarkably like them, even wearing the workers' overalls my friends wore. They were building a house, too, but they weren't being funny about it. In anger, the one who looked like Ollie heaved a brick at the one who looked like Stan. Then the one who looked like Stan began to cry, wringing his hands, kneeling and beating his head against the earth.

I watched their somber antics for some time, marveling at the resemblances, until it dawned on me that these men did not merely look like my friends but, in fact, were my friends themselves as they would be as older men, having aged thirty, forty or fifty years.

I ran back to where my younger friends were still haplessly hammering away, getting it wrong every time. "Stan! Ollie!" I shouted. "You've got to see what I've just seen." We hastened to the place where the older men had been. The house they were building was there, but the men were not around. "Let's look for them," Stan said to Ollie. "Very well, Stanley," Ollie answered. "But see that you don't get us into trouble." Stan and Ollie wandered around looking for their older selves. At some point, though, bored with the search, they took up the older men's tools to work on the house their doubles had abandoned.

It was a joy to see my friends exerting themselves, comically mucking it up at every turn. But when I suggested that the older men had probably left for the day and that we should return home, Stan answered, "I don't know. What do you think, Ollie?" Ollie replied: "I know what you're thinking, Stanley. We should stay and meet these men. I don't know why we know it, but we think this is most important."

We stayed through the night, Stan and Ollie working away at the house, which never seemed any closer to completion. The next day, Ollie told me that I could go home; they'd decided to make an indefinite stay.

"Even if it means waiting thirty, forty or fifty years." said Ollie, Stan by his side, nodding.

AMONG THE DISAPPOINTMENTS OF LOVE

Daisy, wearing the green and orange,
Of her long ago prep school,
Her blond hair faded, mousy,
Looking at me, asking:
"Did you say your name was Seth Thomas?"

"Seth Thomas? The clock maker?"
Well, it had been
A longish time, I suppose,
Since Daisy and I had been together.

She offered to cook dinner for me
At her Village apartment.

"It's a leg of lamb. I cooked it
Myself."

Unveiled, it was bloody. "How long did you cook this?"

"Oh, fifteen minutes, give or take."

I pushed my plate aside.

"I shall read your Tarot cards now,"
She, cards in hand, shuffling, announced.
The first: "The Knight of Wands!"
The second: "The World, reversed!"
And the third: "The Two of Coins!"

But what did they mean?

"They mean," she, indigently,
"Exactly what they say they are!

You can't hide from truth!"

I'd brought no wine;
She offered no water.
We sat silently,
Until three minutes past eight.

"I'm sorry," she sighed.
Her measure
Completing its circle.
"I can't marry you, after all.
Tomorrow I leave
For the Antipodes
Never to return!"

I had not asked her to marry me!

Mortified, outraged, I gorged myself
At a nearby restaurant,
Then returned home
To the clocks ticking loudly,

Despite gorging,
I was starving,
Just starving.

Partial Menu of Dishes Returned to the Kitchen by a Former Girlfriend

—for Tom Pollock

Restaurant	Food or Drink	Reason Returned	Action Taken
Tour d'Argent, Paris	Tour d'Argent Duck #99,487,388, soufflé potatoes	Duck not boned to her liking. Potatoes "kinda mushy"	Reprimanded chef
Banquette, Savoy Hotel, London	Fruit and Custard Trifle	Too "sugary"	Refused to eat
Savoy Grill, Savoy Hotel, London	Lager Ale	Too warm	Scolded bartender
Nathans, Coney Island	Hotdog	Roll "too mushy"	Turned nose up at counterman
Park Bistro, New York City	Crème brûlée	Top "burnt and crisp"	Letter of complaint to management
Mr. Stox Restaurant, Anaheim	Almas Caviar, blini. Whole French Black Winter Truffle – Perigord, in salt Krug, Clos du Mesnil 1995	"Too fishy" "Didn't taste good" Maybe corked	Complained to manager. Outrage and shouting. Banned for life.
French Laundry, Napa	Tasting of Vegetables	"Too stringy"	Chef would not discuss
Masa, New York City	Sushi	"Not fresh enough"	Chef not amused

Victoria & Albert's, Orlando	Roast Beef, Yorkshire Pudding	Beef "not rare enough; also over-cooked." Pudding "soggy" in places, or too firm"	Patiently explained to chef how to cook roast beef and Yorkshire pudding.
Alinea, Chicago	Black Truffle Explosion	Truffle broth burst while she chewed	Chef explained that that was the way it was supposed to happen; she disagreed, predicted someone would soon slip on expelled broth and sue restaurant. Escorted to door.
Seeger's, Atlanta	Eight-course Tasting Menu	Refused to eat; reason undetermined	Passed out drunk in parking lot
Agawama, Tokyo	Kobe Beef Steak	Not "beef-steaky" enough	Ignored
Gordon Ramsay Restaurant, London (Chelsea)	(did not order)		Made insulting comments on decor. Chased into street by owner
Quanjude Roast Duck Restaurant, Beijing	Six Course Peking Duck Dinner	Demanded low sodium soy sauce	Ignored. Refused to eat
The Futurists Banquet, San Francisco	Halibut Stuffed with Ball Bearings	Ball bearings "rusty"	Didn't think that was funny. Blamed me.

OUR 'HOOD

after "Our Village" by Thomas Hood (1799–1845)

"There were scarcely any events in the life of Thomas Hood."
–William Michael Rossetti: *Introduction to the Collected Works of Thomas Hood.*

You find us through a grove of oaks, where slaves were hanged not long ago, and by a stand of willows, under which on summer days, young men and women pose for pornographic videos.

And beyond that is a parking lot so vast, cars are parked and never found.

There's our lake wherein lie drowned the priest and three altar boys, lighted candles by their coffins, haloed faces rippling the swell.

We have eighteen funeral homes in fervid competition. "When may we expect you, Sir? Madam?" is the universal, nervous greeting.

Neighbors steal from neighbors. They exchange possessions, dress and thought. And, so, over the years, have transformed themselves into the people from whom they stole.

Here's the grown-up boy who everyday brings home tricycles, playpens, computers, shopping carts from the supermarket—any old set of discarded things. Each night his father quietly hauls that day's collection to the curb.

Here's our prostitute. The taxi driver used to drive her to assignations. She'd tip him $2.00. Now she's retired, set up in a house down the block. "Afternoon, Sonya!" he calls as she walks past. She squints, bends her head to forty-five degrees. "Twenty dollars!" she calls back, recognizing him from the horizontal.

Our neighbor's house caught fire—something about a cigarette tossed into lighter fluid just to see what would happen. The Fire Department was ready with the hoses, but gaped in silence at the fire, then the captain saying: "It's good we wait to see what happens next."

On Mondays we watch the Perp Walk. Today it's the mayor shackled to the Police

Chief. "Lo Jeremiad!" laments loudly the local crank. "Why did we take all those hallucinogens in the '60s?"

Our hospital sells body parts. Free enterprise has been brisk. Even living patients are missing organs and appendages. "I know I had it when I came in," each thinks.

Our pastor prays in the churchyard: "Oh Lord, who are we kidding? Grant us that we never die, like this poor idiot. What is it you need, oh Lord, to make this work? Storm shutters, a new set of tires? They're yours. Amen."

We remember our casualty from the World Trade Center, his last message on his wife's answering machine: "I'm leaving now. Keep that damn dog out of my tomato plants!"

Here's our athletic field whereupon young boys and girls play a game without ball or puck. The rules say players must bash each other with iron mallets. We are the tri-county champions!

The police tell us if there weren't so many wires coming into our houses our murder rate would triple.

Here's the boy who one day took an electric drill to his brother's head. Caught in the act he swore: "I am an American. I do not torture."

Here's our local newspaper. Today's headline: Cannibals Running Day Care Center! Seventh Banner Year!

Fifteen hit-and-runs last week, twenty-seven so far this week. You get used to the bodies lying there; just step around them.

Now there is only one place I have not told you about in our village, and it is my house. And what goes on in there is none of your goddamned business.

And each night in the high school parking lot, the primal roar and crash of the SUVs as they collide, fall back and collide again under the oceanic tugging of the moon.

TO A FORMER PLAYMATE OF THE MONTH

for Alice Denham

"It's strange," she confides.
"Every night I dream and it's always
The faces of people I've never met, never
Known, never even
Seen."

And I think: For so long
You've been stared at
By adolescents,
Older men
In stale marriages,
Or those too shy to find their own playmate,
Or who've abandoned hope of it
Altogether;
Your body examined minutely
As if you were a butterfly,
Wings pinned
To the lepidopterist's board.

It seems justice
That you get
To study them
Now.

FROM Nathan in the Ancient Language

for Charles A. Matz

1.

"Hey, you," Father called.
"Come feel this new suit of mine,
Coattails, this fabric,
Intricate touch." They fit,
As if he'd been
Born to them,
Not they made to his order.

"Gentlemen of our station"
(He unctuous, purring, instructing)
"Are rightly judged
By texture of clothing, moral
Fiber, by tailor's pattern.
Above all, our Anglican Church:
Always respecting the gentleman's gesture,
Never intruding upon one's
Religious beliefs.

Sundays with him, an oasis
Of admiration by others
Sitting by our side
In tailored elegance. How
Wonderful our reflections
He sun,
I moon.

He died, though,
His coffin lowered
Into earth
On endless rope,
Uncoiling spindle.

We waited days,
Nights
For sound
Of landing. But sound
Came there none.

Eventually, I believed,
He'd come to rest
In China.
He'd open his eyes
And in utter delight
Detect himself arrived
In a country
To his immense liking,
A country
Filled with tailors!

2.

Father gone, I
Found myself in white mountains,
At school in white buildings,
Where snow fell always.
Our jackets and slacks
White,
And we boys of wind-bleached skins,
Light hair, pink eyes,
Some of us tall, towering,
Others small huddling,
Like me.

Friends I found none.
Memory of nameless girl:
Country Club tea dance.
My first, only love gone from me
Aborning.

Winds blew up the valleys
And I was hungry, hungry.
In sleep I cried in

Ancient language, language
Of my father:
"Eala, Faeder   hu fela hyrlinga
on mines fæder   huse half genohne
habbað,   ond ic her on
hunger forweorðe!" And then I would vow:
"Ic arise ond ic   fare to minum fæder
and ic secge him,   'Eala fæder, ic syngode
On heofonas and   beforan þe.
I have sinned on heaven and before you.
Let me back
Into the home of your comfort,
Inspiration! But
The morning drifts
Did not
Abate.

3.

There were giants
In the shower room
In those days, lurching,
Bellowing in primeval
Swamp-shadow.

In corners hid
The youngest, fairest of us
Terrified of monsters
That their scabrous attentions might
Press against us,
Shagging legs and thighs.
Our daily terror
To be caught alone by one.

And I, one afternoon,
Thinking myself safe,
Bathing in a veiling web
Of steam, my chest suddenly encircled
By immense arms
Dragging

Me towards sucking, sweltering maw
Salivating at center.
I, the fly in
Steamy web-strings.

But ere we could reach that point
Someone cried to me,
"Hey, you!"

At once I was freed
And vaguely could see
At the end of the room
My attacker, his arms bound
By white bathrobe cord
Knotted to shower head—he
Flailing under the scalding,
Unable to free himself.

From that fog emerged
Another boy. Not one of the giants,
Someone of middle height I'd seen
Between snowdrifts
Making our way to class.

"Remember me?" asked boy.
"From some
Life ago?"

I, too awed to think, answer.

"Well, then," he plowing through silence.
"I am Nathan. At your service.
Call when you're in need. Anytime,
In remembrance
Of shared past."
He added. "It's my pleasure."
And
Was gone.

Baffled

Yet,
Fearing giant's reprisal
I concentrated,
Survival my mission.

But, strangely, no giants
Appeared to
Startle me.

When next we met,
Nathan explained,
"I've put out the word. They'll
Leave you be."

How he could do this
Was a mystery to me.

4.

Months passed, years.
Our white diplomas
Tossed into air,
Swallowed by snow and bleached
Sky.

"How can I..." stumbling
When Nathan and I met then.

"Think," he said,
"Nothing of it. Perhaps
You'll extend
Help to me
Someday. For
Old times, dark
Times."

What did he mean?
But I promised! Yes, I swore! Of course
I would.

from Part II: Poostie/Malaka

1.

At home, thereafter,
In silent, antique house:
Empty streets to its face,
Vast ocean, beach
To its rear.

Mother
Stern in shadows: anger
Short or long as dream, perpetual
Lightning in coiled night.

Stepfather
Obvious, oblivious,
Ponderous, impervious.
Speaker of
Twelve languages,
Doctorates in Law,
Religion, Medicine,
Mortuary Science.
Perhaps four hundred
Pounds of him in vast
Ungainly costume (our tailor
Refusing the commission.
"I am a tailor," says he.
"I do not drape
Upholstery.")

At bridge table
Mother bids a card:
"You cannot sleep
All summer. You
Must find
Work."

Stepfather bids a card.
"Idleness," he, solemn intones, "Is the soul's rust."

Mother, another card, same suit:
"You must work among the people
To learn you are not
Of their station."

And stepfather:
"Unless it will up and think and taste and see, all is in vain!"

Summer days pass.
Unproductive world
Slogs slower.
Mother, daily, the sound
Of tea cups
Lapping, stepfather—
Vast, vapid,
Lathargic lummox.

Yet, one day, he
Surprises me:
I, hiding in bedroom,
Spy the man
Darkly suited, correct tie,
But on his feet: roller-blades!
He looks left, he looks
Right. Satisfied he is
Alone,
He skates. Makes
Vast circles,
Figure-eights,
Twirls,
Arms outstretched,
Hands sharpened planes
As if escaping gravity,
Abandoning dead weight
Of himself. His body
In grace, now,
Sun reflecting from eyeglasses,
Seeming celestial, almost.
A meteor! A planet!

Round and round he twirls
In space.

2.

Hounded from house
I try work: I dress in coveralls
To move furniture.
I in plaid jacket, bowtie, sell
Encyclopedia
Door-to-door.
In grimy kitchen coat, I
Bus tables.
In sailor suit:
White hat, blouse, trousers.
With a stick I pick
Up cigarettes and trash,
Disgusted.

Finally, I find my place,
My station in life,
The taxi stand.
I adorn my head
In snappy cap. I learn
the streets
("You gotta
Know the streets," says my mentor,
A cabby for life.)

I adore the hours
On the road. I love the little diner
Where each morning at ten
I break for snacks.
(Lovely, luscious Danish, bear claw, donut, coffee cake, miniature pie, jelly sandwich,
five sugars in coffee. I gain thirty-seven pounds.)

The countermen love me.
"Whadda you want, Malaka?"
They ask. I
Flattered, think
"Malaka" means "Kid," "buddy," "pal,"—

Endearments we
Of honest proletariat class
Share with affection.

Then, on rare night shift,
I ask another,
"Just what does this *'Malaka'* mean?
In English, that is?"

"Oh no, no," says he.
"This I cannot tell."

I demand.

"It is bad word. Very bad."

"Well?"

Reluctant. "It means
You are 'jerk-off.'"

Stunned, ashamed. These
Waiters—my friends!
Angered, I plan
Good natured revenge.

"Tell me something in your language
To say back
When they call
me 'Malaka.'"

Embarrassed. At length:
 "Call them 'Poostie'" Then confiding:
"That mean 'ass-fucker.'"

Anon, I meet the morning
Coffee break. "Waddya want,
Malaka?" They ask.

Swift as shadow

I repost: "Gimme a coffee, Poostie!"

Silence among staff. Then raucous
Laughter.
Fingers pointing at waiter.
He flustered, red faced.

Later, after laughter ends,
He whispers in my ear:
"Now I have to kill you!"

It was no joke. I lay broad awaking,
Then fled
From that place.

3.

Headed homeward.
Throw snappy cap from
Car window, abandon
Taxi life
Forever.
"Why do I see you
In the middle of day?"
Demands mother
From shadows.

I cannot confide in her.
I need fatherly advice.
I find stepfather
In library.
He, absolutely motionless,
Black robed,
At the stacks.
He has
Read all the books
Remembers all,
Wistful, now, for blessings
Of dementia
So to read them
Again in innocent

Wonder.

He turns to me—
Pivots, actually,
180 degrees
One fluid motion.

I ask to confide.
He nods. I tell him
The waiter's threat. My
Abiding misery.
I beg
His advice.

He nods his head, pronounces:
"Every man hath a rainy corner of his life whence comes foul weather which follows him."
"But it is worse than that,"
I protest. "The man
Threatened my life!"
Stepfather stroking chin.
Wisdom bearded, reposts:
"He who makes a beast of himself gets rid of the pain of being a man."

"But how am I
To avoid his pursuit? How
Am I to live?"

Stepfather offers:
"A man must swallow a toad every morning if he wishes to be sure of finding nothing
still more disgusting before the day is out."

I, then, barely
Clutching hope
Of his understanding:
"But how am I
To get on with my life?"

He smiles.
"The thought of suicide is a great consolation: with the help of it one has got through
many a bad night."

When I do not react—
Cannot react.
"Woe," says he, "Is wondrously clinging: The clouds ride by."

He pivots
Back to books.
They more
His confidants

Than I.

4.

That waiter: I see him
Everywhere. That must be he,
Parking cars at country
Club. Or he,
In alley behind
Theater—waiting,
Watching me!
Then,
Frightful morning,
I peering through window
See him right there,
Mowing lawn,
Circling closer, closer
To house.
I turn an instant,
Then look back,
And it is his eyes
Staring at me
From outside
Window! Staring
At me through
Glass in door.

I, in flannel
Pajamas, begin abode
Beneath my bed.
Little can bring me out
Save servants set

For me a good
Dinner in kitchen. I
Do not hover
At windows.
Neither do I venture out of
Doors. There is
No escape! I will myself
To become
Dust beneath
My bed.

5.

By dusty light
From window
I read my favorite books,
Loved by me
From school days,
My boyhood's solitary
Companion.
The author: B.F. Turley from England.
His hero: Topsy Sidebottom,
Young English earl,
And Vasquez,
His omniscient valet,
Vasquez
Who saves his master
Innumerable times
From folly.
I knew from first reading
That I am Topsy. He
Is me. Our fortunes
Identical.

Hours
Of hidden pleasure
Beneath the bed,
But sadness, too.

But then, hurrah!
Huzzah!
A letter

From long-lost
Nathan,
Savior from school
Days.

"Hey you!" he writes
"I arrive at airport
Tuesday next.
Meet me there. Old
Times! Good
Times!"

He's come
To deliver me from travail—I can
Feel it.

6.

Liberating day it is! I decide
To walk outside, our little park.
I dress in new plus-fours,
Pork pie hat—a gentleman's costume.
And then
Out the door and across
The bridge
Where picnickers
Disport.

I spy
A family, it seems:
Children, wife, husband,
His back to me.

"Hello!" I cheer them
Husband turns.
My horrors! It is
The waiter.

He rises,
Stalks me,
Forces me back

To bridge, his face
Constricted
In hate rictus.

"You stupid *Malaka-Poostie!*
You jerk-off ass-fucker!"
He curls his hand into fist.

Reason with him, explain:
"What I said. It
Was meant
A joke. Shake
Hands like gentlemen.
Be friends."

But reason finds
No home. He shouts:
"Listen to me!
You don't insult me
In my language!
My own words
That belong to me! You
Cannot take away
My right: My words!
Now I kill you. I
Throw you off bridge
And I kill you!"

He drags me to railing,
Grasps my neck
With ham hands,
Butts his head
Into my face.

I behave then... oddly.
Grab his hand,
Twist. His
Leaves my neck.
Force him to
Turn. It is his neck

Grasped by my
Hand now.

"Now you kill me!" he puffs.
"You are man? You do it!"

But not I,
A killer.

"You don't kill me?" he
Gasps. "You don't kill me,
You *Poostie-Malaka?*"

What to do?
Then, inspiration.
"Promise, never
To bother me again. Then
I let you go."

"I promise you nothing!"
Waiter, contorted,
Screams.

I compromise:
"I trust you," I pledge.
"I will
Let you go.
See you keep out of my way
Or else more of this!"
(I squeeze neck
With my hand.)

The man, silent.
I push him
Away. But
He does not retreat. He
Turns, shoves me,
Forces me to ground,
Leaps on me, pins my legs
With his legs,

My shoulders
With his hands.

"You stupid *Poostie*!" shreiks
He. "You spit my words back
At me? Here I spit out yours!"
A terrible retching:
He spits
Horrible sputum
Onto my face.

Consumed, confused,
Cowardly, I say
Nothing.

He stands. His
Malediction: "You
Never change.
You always
Be *Poostie-Malaka.*"

Then turns:
"Now you do
What I say. What
I tell you. You
The waiter now.
You wait on me!
The future!" he exclaims.
"I will enjoy
The future-with
You!"

Troubling,
His words. I
Retreat home.
Safety under
Bed. More
Topsy Sidebottom
Adventures to read,

His brilliant
Valet Vasquez,
Who
Always
Saves his master.

✹

7.

And then, days
Later, sun
On bedroom floor
Burning me
As if in hell.
Have to get
Air, no matter
The risk.
To the beach,
That horrible place.
Just behind our house.

Sky blinding white,
I slog through wet sand
Desperate
For cure. But what? As if I knew
But could not voice it.

And then came voices
To me
From nearby. A sacrad
Melody. And found
At end of sand
A choir
At rehearsal,
Melodious.

Young minister, abstracted,
Leaning against church door.
"Are you here to sing,
To join the choir?"

I look into church. Men,
Women voicing hymn,
Wearing... wearing...
Something wonderful! Vestments!
Red cassock! Frilly white
Surplice!
Revelation:
My cure, as always,
A change
Of costume! But
How to affect this?

'You must join the choir!' minister
Proclaims, answering
Furtive thoughts.

"I will," I cry. "I will make
A joyful noise
Unto the Lord!"

Minister beaming,
Enrobes me. I raise my hand
Above him,
I, Archangel, in red cassock, frilly
White surplice make
Magic signs, semaphores.
I am inspired. I intone my revelation:
My joyful noise.
"Ute! Ute! Ute!" I
Howl as ancient warriors
Of my family howled: *"Ute! Ute! Ute!"*

I run into sunlight, a
Wind blowing
Filling vestments
My angel's wings,
I, gliding through dunes
My journey homeward.

Sunbathers watch.

I raise my arms, trace
Magic benediction, my eyes radiating
Inner Light, intoning from depths
Of soul: *"Ute! Ute! Ute!*
Ute! Ute! Ute!
Amen! Amen! Amen!"

Breathless, I return
Via back door, stealth, mystic
Revelation uncompromised, unseen
Skulking I,
To bedroom.

8.

It is the appointed day
The hour.
I, at our little airport
Watching
Sky.

We'd heard
(We corresponding old school friends)
That Nathan became a hero
In war,
Flying bombers
Bravely!
Would he arrive in his jet?
Streaming white tracer plumes?
Something glorious
Beyond doubt, I was sure.

But no plane appears.

"No scheduled flights," airport
Official informs.

I'm saddened, of course, ready
For home. But then, silver
Bus pulls up. Stops.
Door

Opens. Passengers exit. Then
Driver, leather flight jacket,
Gallant military cap tilted
Roguishly, manifest in hand,
Swings to ground
Through metal doors.

And "Hey you!" from him.
It is Nathan!

I greet him, of course,
Effusively. But why this bus?

"You've got to drive
Something," says he,
No further explanation
Offered.

He declares:
"I've had a revelation. Thought
I could bunk with you
A few days—back to
The old neighborhood.
To work it out. You know,"
Think I: *Old neighborhood?*
Has he been here before? I cannot
Recall. Did I
Know him before? Not
Possible!

But, yet, what coincidence! Nathan's
Revelation. And I've had
Revelation, too:
My vestments,
My *"Ute! Ute! Ute!"*
I'm in rush to tell him about it, but
He lifts his hand: "In good
Time," he calms. "Soon."

At home, I diffident

Asking mother
Her leave for him to stay.

She comes forth from
Shadows, inspects Nathan. Actually
Smiles. "Of course your friend can stay,"
She says. "We have known him
For a long, long
Time...."

I am
Flabbergasted.

10.

Mother dotes on Nathan, has
Tailor fit him
New clothes. Speaks to him
In motherly manner.
I would be jealous, brood, except
I'm preoccupied:
Damn waiter shows up
At back door every
Day. Takes me off guard.
"Today," says he,
"I bring my family. We sit beneath
Shady tree. You
Bring us nice picnic basket."

Well, I think, not a big request.
Wouldn't want him to be hungry,
Go away angry.

I direct Cook see to it. I
Watch from window. They eat,
Drink, leave everything on lawn,
Garbage, dirty plates, knives,
Spoons, glasses. Well,
He's not a very nice person, I

Think.

Next week: he's back.
"You pay me one hundred dollars. I
Protect your house."

"Why?" I demand. "What could
happen?"

"Many thieves, vandals. You see."

"No," I tell him. Got to stand up
To him. "No."

"Ah, then, you see, *Malaka*. I go away,
Then something bad happens."

He goes. Then glass breaks.
Window!
Big rock on carpeted floor.
He's back. "I told you. You need
Protection. Give me one hundred dollars."

Perhaps he's right. I give it him. He goes.
Nothing happens
Thereafter
For rest of day.

Except next day, he
Returns. Again,
Then again. Each day. More
Money, more food, more
Threats.

I keep this hidden from family,
From Nathan. Too embarrassing,
Humiliating.

At length, another
Demand, this one

Too much:
"Tonight I bring my friends. Maybe midnight.
Maybe later.
You bring us food, beer. We make music.
We dance. We make loud party. You stay away. You
Watch from window,. he points
To my bedroom window. "You see
How real men dance!"

"You can't do it," I declare. "There are laws,
Ordinances, you see. There are (and now I finish
Weakly) 'family considerations." (How
Could I keep this orgy
From family's sight
And hearing—from Nathan's—
At such late hour?)
"Hey you, *Malaka*! I do it because
I can. And you do it
Because I say you must.
We be here at midnight, or after."

I fret, ring hands.
How avoid disaster? I
Invent one hundred solutions.
None can work. Finally,
My only recourse: I consult
Nathan.

11.

I confess everything.
He laughs!
"That's '*Malaka*' he calls you? What a riot!"

I steam under laughter.
"What then," I beg.
"What shall I do to prevent
Disaster?"

He is quiet.
Eyes half closed. Hands

Circling above head
In magical motions
Then:
"You do not prevent it. You sponsor it!
You welcome it! You exalt in it!
Invite them over for a gala!
Supposed disaster for one, means,
Disaster for other."

His meaning escapes
me.

"You just do it."
Reluctantly,
I agree. I have two masters now,
None of which is me.

12.

Next day I give orders for
Food to feed
Interlopers. Nathan
Assures: "Give them beer. Plenty
Of wine. Encourage them
To dance."

My directions acted upon by servants,
Bustle of preparations. But where is mother?
Stepfather? Much goes on
Loud noises, orders shouted,
Great tubs of beer, wine,
Set in place, but
Mother never asks—not
A word.

Meanwhile, Nathan
All day
Down the beach with shovel,
Naked big arms scooping sand,
A deep hole. Why?
All day I stand with him, he

Won't talk, not a word. Just
Smiles as if at some private ecstasy.
Teasing me? Digging to China
Finding my father, maybe.

I wait long hours. Then midnight
These creatures—hated waiter And his others—thirty men show up,
Rowdy, drunk already.
The food, drink set
Before them. Light bonfires,
     Driftwood, seaweed fueled.
     They cheer vulgar luxury,
Whoop, guzzle beer, stuff
Mouth maws, shout
Toasts in foreign
Tongue.

I, at window, watching.
Men dance in sand, circling,
Holding hands,
Others playing stringed instruments.
Two drumming
Rhythm for their dance. Cavorting
Shadows, monstrous, climb
High walls of my house.

Hours pass. Moon is gone. Weak
Starlight. I can see
Men lying in sand.
Sleeping
Drunken sleep. Others still
Dancing, drinking, shouting fighting,
Finally fall
Unconscious.

Fires die. Nothing moves
But wind and waves. I sleep, too, but
Wake hearing screams, men shouting
In pain. A pounding sound, a
Pummeling, battering. I

Frightend under bed,
Wait. And soon, piecemeal,
The screamers' silenced. Then
Stillness once again.

Morning comes soon. Beach white fog,
Ocean white foam. Sun
Pale white disk. I see discarded
Muddy clothes, broken crockery. Party ruins.
But men have gone, gone
Home? There is

Much to clean.

13.

I wander house, look
For Nathan. Find him with stepfather.

"Hey, you!" Nathan greets.
"Some party
You threw
Last night!"

Stepfather immobile.

"I heard screaming, men,
Crying, groaning. And then, at morning, all gone."

"Yes," says Nathan. "It is a mystery, these things."

"And what about the gaping gap
You dug in sand? That gone, too."

Nathan says nothing.

Stepfather turns,
Suddenly, deafeningly shouts: *"Hwæt!*
Hwæt! Wē Gárdena   in géardagum
þéodcyninga   þrym gefrúnon·
hú ðá æpelingas   ellen fremedon!"

I recognize Ancient Language, language of
My father. Baffled, I turn
To Nathan.
He grinning, says, "Your stepfather is about to tell you
What happened in the night.
Listen up!
I shall translate."

Stepfather:
"*Gewat ða neosian*   *syþðan niht becom,*
hean huse   *hu hit Hring-Dene*
æfter beorþege   *gebun hæfdon.*"

Nathan:
"Then Grendel prowled,   palled in darkness,
The sleep-warm hall   to see the Ring-Danes
After beer and feasting   bedded down for rest."

Stepfather:
"*Fand þa ðær inne*   *æþelinga gedriht*
Swefan æfter symble   *sorge ne cuðon,*
Wonsceaft wera.   *Wiht unhælo,*
Grim ond grædig.   *gearo sona wæs,*"

Nathan:
"He found inside   slumbering warriors
Unready for murder.   Bereft of remorse
From love exiled   lost and graceless
He growled with envy   glared about them
Towering with rage."

Stepfather:
"*Reoc ond reþe*   *ond on ræste genam*
þritig þegna   *þanon eft gewat*
Huðe hremig   *to ham faran,*
Mid þære wælfylle   *wica neosan.*
Ða wæs on uhtan   *mid ærdæge*
Grendles guðcræft   *gumum undyrne*
þa wæs æfter wiste   *wop up ahafen,*
Micel morgensweg."

Nathan:
"From their rest   he snared
Thirty hall-thanes   loped howling away
Gloating with corpses   galloping the moors
Back to his cavern   for a cold banquet."

It was too much. Stunned
But ever curious,
I ask Nathan:
"How do you know
The old language? You are
Not, properly speaking
A member of this family."

"*Hwæt*! Listen to me!"   Nathan in whisper.
"Those are my words.   My own words that
belong to me!   That are my right:
My words!"

And I surmise, in later days.
What this Grendel, this Nathan
Has that night done.

New Poems

RAVENOUS

I'd fumbled along with poetry
for years, poisoned
by an early success: a book
published by a college
when I was twenty. Too early,
really. Just a lot of imitations.
Unmasked by James Tate at Columbia University,
the M.F.A. program, ("All your poems are imitations of mine!")
—Well, not entirely. I did imitate others,
such as my mentor, David Ignatow.

He was a well-established poet when we met,
with a 72-page collection of his poems published
every few years
by Wesleyan University Press.
("You're a freak," Tate damned me. "A WASP Ignatow!")

I'd show David my poems. After that first book
I couldn't please him. "These are shit," he'd tell me,
then go on to praise some ditty
I'd scribbled on a cocktail napkin.

The wilderness years.
 I couldn't find her:
Poetry, the halo-haired girlfriend
who leaves the note on your refrigerator:
"I'll be back in a decade or so. Don't hold dinner."

But then, years later, she does return!
or at least my poetry begins to make sense to me.
How strange, and how late in the day.
"Make me some dinner!" she demands. "I'm ravenous!"

So I write and write.

Halloween

My old teacher's wife, once a lovely being,
suffered from sudden hallucinatory rages.

I took a friend
along with me.

She opened her battered apartment door.
Unkempt hair,
torn dress, face smeared
with bizarre orangey blush,
the apartment in dark disarray,
a few sputtering candles the only light.

She smiled when she recognized me
but when she noticed my friend.
her mouth opened wide, a cavern of anger,
her speech slurred without dentures,
her face turning a deeper orange, eyes wide—
a jack-o-lantern mask.

"Who" she screamed, "have you brought
to molest me?"

I turned to my friend, a psychologist, about to apologize,
but watched as his face changed, too:
assuming the mask
of the clinical,
distant
hospital professional.

"I am the nightmare!" she shouted at him.
"Who are you?"

"I am

the doctor."

INNOCENCE

When I was young, our pastor preached a sermon that caught my attention. "You know," he told us. "If Jesus was being put to death today we'd be worshipping an Electric Chair up there on the altar instead of the Cross."

I imagined Jesus superimposed on all the movies I'd seen that featured electrocution. The poor man! His head shaved, strapped in the chair, and 10,000 volts coursing through him! Would he beg the prison screws to spare his life, as James Cagney had done in that film? When the switch was thrown would his head explode, as I'd seen happen in horror movies? And rising again after death—he'd look pretty ragged, probably scare his apostles into apostasy!

Now, of course, we have Lethal Injection and the platform on which it is performed is in the shape of the Cross.

We find this device a familiar comfort, as when we first sang praises to the Lord on those innocent Sunday mornings when I was young.

TEN ENGULFED CATHEDRALS

Accompaniment to La cathédrale engloutie, by Claude Debussy

—for Cathy Callis

La cathédrale engloutie, an ancient Breton myth in which a cathedral, submerged underwater off the coast of the Island of Ys, rises up from the sea on clear mornings when the water is transparent. Sounds can be heard of priests chanting, bells chiming, and the organ playing across the sea.

1. This is the cathedral of the penitents, prostrate before their bishop. The air is choking with incense and though they are cleansed and holy, they're sneaking glances beneath the pews, grasping for light from opaque windows, sniffing for hope in the impenetrable smoky curtain—desperately looking for the way out.

2. This is the cathedral of the Eternal Feast, as painted by Pieter Bruegal, the Elder. The ravenous monks and nuns eat day and night. There is never enough to satisfy them! They are born at table, grow old and die, and are consumed there the next meal. No one is sated and no one pushes away with a satisfied belch!

3. This is the cathedral of the insects. Although in holy robes, there is nothing human about them. They streak from pillar to pole like neurons in the brain, their own agenda compelling them onward. Their mission only to their Holy Queen cosseted deep in the cathedral's reliquary. Foreign to us as are our own thoughts, there is nothing we can learn from them.

4. This is the cathedral where Martin Luther's *Ninety-Five Theses* are nailed to the door. This is the cathedral of confrontation and blame, the cathedral where wrongs are righted only to be wronged. The cathedral of the Inquisition, its pliers, its garrotes. This is the cathedral of endless argument and vexation, of contrition that unfolds the mawkish banner of arrogance.

5. This is the cathedral of sunlight through stained glass, of pleasant weather—the day we believed would go on forever! But this cathedral will also sink into the sea, water pouring in through the springtime open windows, too soon, "'Till Human voices wake us and we drown."

6. This cathedral rises to giddy heights, its choirs singing hallelujahs, caught in

the rapture of the moment, cradling us in ecstatic embrace. But, inevitably this cathedral sinks, its voices one by one, like fireworks falling into water, extinguished. And then we are alone with the dreary necessities: setting bread and cheese on the lonely dinner table.

7. This is the cathedral in which everything is cataloged—-candle holders, patens, chalices, incense, relics of saints, crucifixes, vestments and Gospels. This is the church of learning, of order, and of the Scriptorium where all these things are written down.

8. In the dome of this cathedral, Michelangelo is painting the ceiling. He's embedding messages of brotherhood, tolerance, and freethinking, but artfully, so that the archbishop will not know he is abandoning church dogma. This is his passionate secret and ours. He is absorbed in his realization as we are absorbed in him.

9. This is the cathedral where there are finally gifts worth giving, where sermons make sense, and answers are worth hearing. This is also the cathedral of the quotidian. In this place, *chacun passe, / chacun vient, chacun va.* But there is hope, and order, and determination—proof that we can do better.

10. This is the cathedral of all cathedrals in which the hell-bound, the hungry, the insects, the angry, the tranquil, the rapturous, the learned, the realized, and those with aspirations are assembled, a tableaux in the cathedral's shadowbox. The priests are chanting, the bells are chiming, and the organ is playing. We hear it across the sea, a vision engulfed by clouds.

RECONSTRUCTION OF A LOST POEM
BY ARMAND SCHWERNER

When I read my poetry aloud, the air
fills with light and fireflies, and
it is summer 1970 in The Springs, East Hampton
where the rents are almost cheap
and you can take a leak on the lawn
with impunity
and feel that you
own the place.

But when you read *your* poetry aloud, the air
fills with moths and
my chair impinges on my ass
and I am annoyed.
I don't like this place—The Springs, East Hampton
thirty years later—and you for a guide,
I am not jealous because you are alive
and I am not. It is just that the rents are impossibly high,
and it takes forever on the crowded highway
from the city, and
you are never alone.

You are the oracle of an unpleasant future, McIntosh.
And I am the oracle of a most pleasant past.
You should quit reading your poetry aloud
and listen to mine, instead.

SESTINA: AGAINST THE PAINTED CORPSE

What is this notion we have about preserving the lifeless body
As it was in life? Is it our natural reaction against the personal sentence of death—embalmed
Remains, the defiance of mortality? Or is its sole purpose to honor the ones we loved?
Is it some deep spiritual urging or some baser emotional thing—
This impulse to erase the final travail on the face of the deceased by the painted
Lips, hands, the eyes closed in seeming peace. Is this the archetypal scheme?

Screw the Egyptians! Go back further: The earliest embalming scheme
Appears in the Etruscan body
Of codices (compiled by Prof. Schwerner) first painted
On cave walls. A little-known tribe embalmed
Their dead with sweet water, soup or some such thing
And posed them at table, slurping the meal that, in life, they most loved.

And Romans posed their dead as lovers or as loved,
As they were in life: in the act or scheme
Of bedding the man, the woman (or, possibly some mechanical thing).
A tribute to vitality, to effulgent soul, supple body
The hope we all share, embalmed
In our longing for this life—this one life!—All sorrows to remain un-painted.

But let's get down to cases. My first view of the Painted
Corpse was that of my uncle James. He loved
Money and, in fact, had his swimming pool embalmed
(As it were) with silver dollars encrusted into its cement sides; a scheme
Made mockery by death on his first swim: his body,
Floating bloated, his swimsuit askew, exposing his shriveled thing.

But, fixed up in a titanium coffin (a thing
Guaranteed never to decay), his pasty painted
Face, hands joined across his body
His morning coat, collar mounting firmly to the chin—as he loved
To dress! This artificial thing, embalmed,
Would rest eternal until Resurrection, that most formal, if perhaps imaginary scheme.

Then, through my life in quick succession, a parade of relatives embalmed:
An aunt, and then another, and then my father, each transformed into this scary thing:
This dead one not really dead, but only sleeping, thanks to mortician's scheme.
In nightmares they would chase me, grotesque visions, purple-painted
Dreams, obliterating true memories of those I had loved
Compressing their individuality into something packaged, a sameness: Out of many, one.

A body not embalmed, after a day or two, may still be recognized and loved,
Appearing only slightly green—not a bad thing, really, with features left un-painted,
Body clothed and accessorized to complete a natural, peaceful aesthetic scheme.

Alarm Clocks

Tom had a problem waking up for work. He, unable to catch the train, getting to the office late every day, always getting fired. But a solution. "I'll sleep in my underwear on the wooden floor surrounded by alarm clocks, each going off five minutes after the last!"

We lived in a tiny community, the distance between bungalows about one foot. The first morning Tom slept through the alarms, cacophony loud enough to anger neighbors, who banged on their walls, some even on our front door.

But Tom's sleep was opaque.
"What time is it?" And then, "Oh damn it to hell, I missed the train!"
Another late arrival, another lost job.

When awake, Tom's eyes darted around nervously as if he were looking for something he couldn't identify. "Well, maybe I'm not looking for the right job or something. Maybe if I found the right thing everything would be okay."

What is it that throws a person so off balance? Tom was an orphan, but I didn't see the connection for several years. We had moved to different cities.

One day he showed up, introduced me to his wife, also an orphan, and to his two children. They smiled. Tom had a good job and was never late for work. His nervous glances had disappeared.

"So you found the right thing?"

"Yes," he replied. "Yes I did."

Norse Mythology

1. *The Forests Surrounding the City of Oslo*

Seen from the air, the forests surrounding the city of Oslo are immense, green, solitary. This is how it must have looked when trees ruled the earth.

The people in the city of Oslo are blond, good humored, friendly. Once in awhile, though, they stop, turn their heads, listen intently

as if anticipating an advance of something primal, inevitable.

2. *Sheepish*

In Geilo, a Norwegian ski resort we mistakenly visited in summer because the prices were low, there were few humans—certainly no skiers—but there were sheep. I encountered five on a hike up the mountain. We stared at each other, then ran away, I as sheepish as they.

Later I met them again, offered each a lettuce leaf I'd brought. Soon we were sitting, munching lettuce. Then they lay against me to nap.

It was cold on the mountain, but I was happy to nap with them under the sheepskin.

3. *My old professor has a bottle of scotch*

We pour drinks and settle back to watch Norwegian TV. But it is all in Norwegian! So we drink and supply our own dialogue.

Here is a woman shouting at a man. The professor ad libs: "It was the squirrel you hid in the closet."

"No," the man answers in my voice. "It was the stranger you hid between the sheets!" Then another man enters shouting dramatically. "Give me the squirrel or give me your wife!"

I rejoin, "Take my squirrel, please!"
"But I want your wife!"

We're both drunk and nodding. "I want your wife!" whispers the professor.

I think he's asleep but he opens his eyes, looks at me, says soberly:

"I want your wife."

4. *Customs*

In Norway, brides wear wedding rings on their right hands.
When people want to call you an asshole
they touch their thumbs with their forefingers
and wave them at your face.

My old professor was driving us timidly on a one-lane country road
after our friends' wedding. Horns behind blasted—the bride and groom wanted to pass!—
but the old man held his place in the road.

When finely the road widened and the bridal party shot by, the bride stuck her right hand
out the passenger window, her thumb and forefinger touching and waving at him.

"Please let me drive," I begged. "You're holding back traffic."

"Why do you say that?" he answered with a smile. "She's giving me the "Ring" sign
She loves me!"

Four Problems of Translation

I. A Lecture from the Bartender at Grand Hotel, Oslo

Translation is difficult. We don't expect our American tourists to speak Norwegian so we learn English. One language can do violence to the other. Pick its pocket, so to speak.

For instance, Oslo gets many meters of snowfall. Knut Hamsun, in *Hunger*, has his character sleeping in the snowed-in streets of Kristiania. (Oslo used to be Kristiania in 1899.) Hamsun knew those streets. But then your Robert Bly comes along with his egregious English translation and messes up the map so that it neither resembles Kristiania nor Oslo. A tourist could get lost in the snow and die following Mr. Bly's map! Knut Hamsun was our breakthrough novelist and maybe deserves more respect, though he was often down and out.

Henrik Ibsen was our breakthrough dramatist—hardly down and out!—but you wouldn't know it from the English translations.

For instance, in *Ghosts*, Mrs. Alving refers to her husband lying around reading "bank journals," which doesn't make any sense in English. But Norwegians know instantly that "bank journals" really means "pornography."

Ibsen drank and dined at the Cafe every night. His dinner was always an open sandwich, beer and schnapps. And often a *pjolter*, which is our word for Whisky and Soda.

And he could get drunk!

Hamsun and Ibsen lived here in Kristiania at the same time, and I think they met only once, poverty and wealth being discrete languages.

One night Ibsen was too drunk to sit. He insulted the waiters and we had to translate him into the street.

Hamsun was down and out, living in a wooden crate outside the Cafe. Ibsen landed next to him and decided to take a little nap. Then you could see Hamsun's arm reach out of the box and pick Ibsen's pocket!

Then Hamsun translated himself into the Cafe and ordered a splendid supper!

II. James Boswell's *Life of Samuel Johnson,* LL.D. published in 1791

They meet at a bookstore, but it doesn't go well. Boswell: "I apologize for being a Scot. I cannot help it." Johnson: "That, Sir, I find, is what a very great many of your countrymen cannot help."

See "Bozzy" of a morning enjoying a public hanging, darting down an alley for quick sex, and later, a fervid night in public or private house playing the buffoon or worse, worse for drink. How could this besotted poltroon produce such a work of light and intelligence?

Well, Macaulay says in 1831, that dolt didn't exactly write the Life, he merely took it down: faithful, mindless stenographer. The Biography has merits, he concludes, but only a fool could have written it.

Later, though, attics and closets of Boswell descendants in Scotland and Ireland open. Manuscript caches take flight, caught up by the universities. Boswell is recognized an exigent writer, not at all vapid, prepared by life for the great work, the superb Biography.

Johnson, moral and intellectual touchstone, now slumps in a grubby corner, mistranslated into something else: Hapless literary marionette.

"Do us a little dance, will ye?" leers lubricious Bozzy.

Johnson arises, clears his throat—ever ready with a pithy quotation.

III. Goethe Writes *Aus meinem Leben:*
Dichtung und Wahrheit (1811–1833)

Goethe's friends entreat him to write the autobiography. One friend: "We try to guess many a riddle, to solve many a problem." But they've reached an impasse. They beg him: "Yet a little assistance here and there would not be unacceptable." "This desire," writes Goethe, "so kindly expressed, immediately awakened within me an inclination to comply with it." But how? One cannot simply write *everything* that has happened. One needs method. "It must be a very agreeable and a re-animating task to treat former creations as new matter, and work them up into a kind of Last Part." He cannot include everything, so he selects incidents, compresses or expands others, eliminates many.

He feels the danger, diddling with history, but he has an honest end to achieve. He declares the title of his autobiography: *Dichtung und Wahrheit, Poetry and Truth.*

Immediately, it is misconstrued in the press. *Dichtung* is understood as meaning

Fiction. "What has Goethe given us?" they ask. "Is it part fiction, part truth? And indeed, which part is which?"

"No, no, no!" Goethe screams. [I translate freely here.] "It was my endeavor to present and express to the best of my ability the actual basic truths that controlled my life as I understood them." The work is translated into English as *Lies and Truth in My Life*. "*Scheiße Kopf!*" shrieks Goethe [in my free translation]. "*Lies?* Are they all idiots? I wanted the word *Dichtung* understood not in the sense of fabrication but as the revelation of higher truths. Doesn't anyone see this?"

"They say your novel, *The Sorrows of Young Werther* is secretly autobiography," I tell him. "But that was a fiction!" he protests. "Certainly the structure contains autobiographical elements, but I made everything else up!" "Well," I say. "Maybe it was easier reading. I mean, after all, your autobiography is, what? Thirteen volumes?" He answers: "That's what you need to get to the truth." And I suggest: "Possibly *Young Werther* is what you need
to get to the poetry."

"Ach," he shakes his head. "Perhaps we shall never resolve this."

"Well then," I say, stretching after a long sit down. "*Möchten Sie ein paar Bier trinken?* Would you like to drink a few beers?"

"*Ja. Natürlich.* A brilliant idea! *Wir zu den Biergarten gehen.*"

Arm in arm we stroll to the beer garden, and as we stroll we sing: *Du, du liegst mir im Herzen,* the song about the man whose heart breaks because his great love cannot take him seriously.

IV. According to My Mother (6)

My mother was frightened. It had been
fifty years since she'd visited the home country.
"I don't think I remember the language!" she fretted.
But she got on the airplane, an old woman
pacing the runway hesitantly.

We heard nothing from her for a month.
Then a telegram: "Returning tonight."

We were surprised when we saw her: her face radiant,

her steps full of life.
"It was a wonderful trip," she gushed
as we drove away in the car.
"At first I couldn't communicate with my family.
But, after awhile, I began to remember the words.

"They took me on a trip, smuggling contraband—radios and such,
over the border. But on the return
the Communists pulled us over. They told us to get out of the car.
They were going to arrest us, put us in their dungeon.
But I pulled out my passport and shouted that I was an American!
and demanded to see the ambassador. Then
I swore at them in Hungarian. (Hungarian has so many
more curse words than English. Really filthy ones!" she chortled.)

She was indeed exuberant, seemingly thirty years younger, as if freed
from the manacles of America and its limited language.

"They backed down and let us go. They tried to threaten me,
but I gave them another piece of my mind
in a language I knew
they damn well understood!"

About the Author

SANDY MCINTOSH was born in Rockville Centre, New York, and received a BA from Southampton College in 1970, an MFA from Columbia University in 1972, and a Ph.D. from the Union Graduate School in 1979. After working with children for eight years as a writer in the schools he completed a study of writers who taught in the program and how their work with children affected their own writing. The study, *The Poets in the Poets-in-the Schools* was published by the Minnesota Center for Social Research, University of Minnesota. He alternated teaching creative writing at Southampton College, New York Institute of Technology, and Hofstra University with publishing nonfiction works, such as *Firing Back* (John Wiley 1997), and computer software, such as *Mavis Beacon Teaches Typing!* (Electronic Arts, 1986). For several years he contributed journalism, poetry, and opinion columns to *The New York Times, Newsday, The Nation, The Wall Street Journal, American Book Review,* and elsewhere. He was also editor and publisher of *Wok Talk,* a Chinese cooking bi-monthly and the author and editor of several Chinese cook books.

His first collection of poetry, *Earth Works,* was published by Southampton College the year he graduated. He has since published seven more collections. His original poetry in a screenplay shared the Silver Medal in the Film Festival of the Americas. The title poem of this collection was published by *The New York Times'* web edition. An excerpt of his collaboration with Denise Duhamel appears on *The Best American Poetry* blog.

He served as chairman of the Distinguished Poets series at Guild Hall, East Hampton, NY from 1980–2000. He was elected to PEN American Center in the 1990s. His biography appears in Contemporary Authors volumes 45–48 (Gale Research Company).

He has been managing editor of Long Island University's national literary journal, *Confrontation*, and is publisher of Marsh Hawk Press.

Titles From Marsh Hawk Press

Jane Augustine, *A Woman's Guide to Mountain Climbing, Night Lights, Arbor Vitae*

Sigman Byrd, *Under the Wanderer's Star*

Patricia Carlin, *Quantum Jitters, Original Green*

Claudia Carlson, *The Elephant House*

Meredith Cole, *Miniatures*

Neil de la Flor, *Almost Dorothy*

Chard deNiord, *Sharp Golden Thorn*

Sharon Dolin, *Serious Pink*

Steve Fellner, *The Weary World Rejoices, Blind Date with Cavafy*

Thomas Fink, *Peace Conference, Clarity and Other Poems, After Taxes, Gossip: A Book of Poems*

Norman Finkelstein, *Inside the Ghost Factory, Passing Over*

Edward Foster, *Dire Straits, The Beginning of Sorrows, What He Ought to Know, Mahrem: Things Men Should Do for Men*

Paolo Javier, *The Feeling Is Actual*

Burt Kimmelman, *Somehow*

Burt Kimmelman and Fred Caruso, *The Pond at Cape May Point*

Basil King, *77 Beasts: Basil King's Bestiary, Mirage*

Martha King, *Imperfect Fit*

Phillip Lopate, *At the End of the Day: Selected Poems and An Introductory Essay*

Mary Mackey, *Sugar Zone, Breaking the Fever*

Sandy McIntosh, *Ernesta, in the Style of the Flamenco, Forty-Nine Guaranteed Ways to Escape Death, The After-Death History of My Mother, Between Earth and Sky*

Stephen Paul Miller, *There's Only One God and You're Not It, Fort Dad, The Bee Flies in May, Skinny Eighth Avenue*

Daniel Morris, *If Not for the Courage, Bryce Passage*

Sharon Olinka, *The Good City*

Justin Petropoulos, *Eminent Domain*

Paul Pines, *Divine Madness, Last Call at the Tin Palace*

Jacquelyn Pope, *Watermark*

Karin Randolph, *Either She Was*

Rochelle Ratner, *Ben Casey Days, Balancing Acts, House and Home*

Michael Rerick, *In Ways Impossible to Fold*

Corrine Robins, *Facing It: New and Selected Poems, Today's Menu, One Thousand Years*

Eileen R. Tabios, *The Thorn Rosary: Selected Prose Poems and New (1998-2010), The Light Sang As It Left Your Eyes: Our Autobiography, I Take Thee, English, for My Beloved, Reproductions of the Empty Flagpole*

Eileen R. Tabios and j/j hastain, *the relational elations of ORPHANED ALGEBRA*

Susan Terris, *Natural Defenses*

Madeline Tiger, *Birds of Sorrow and Joy*

Harriet Zinnes, *Weather Is Whether, Light Light or the Curvature of the Earth, Whither Nonstopping, Drawing on the Wall*

For more information, please go to: http://www.marshhawkpress.org.